The American Book of Changes

Ien Nivens

ISBN-10: 0615952275
ISBN-13: 978-0615952277

To Michelle, who joyously embodies so many qualities of heart and mind that elude my earnest seeking. Your patience comforts me. Your unflagging support and encouragement fortify me.
Always.

CONTENTS

ACKNOWLEDGMENTS

Sarah Sutro's detailed, gentle and insightful reading of this work has proven invaluable. She has pulled more than one hexagram out of the fire and set it back on the anvil for me. I am grateful, and the work is better for it. The support and encouragement of Martin Case, Casey Hickey and Linda O'Brien have buoyed me, especially during the final stages of the manuscript, and Ian Hickey's imagination and enthusiasm have breathed new life into the project that promises to extend it far beyond the pages of this book. Thanks also to Keith Bona for his patience and skill in making its incarnation possible and presentable.

By replacing the tropes of ancient Chinese religion and philosophy that most versions of the I Ching attempt to preserve and explain, I have broken with a tradition to which I am nevertheless deeply indebted. Without the painstaking work of scholars and translators like Richard Wilhelm and C. F. Baynes, Hua Ching Ni, Alfred Huang, Stephen Karcher, and Thomas Cleary (to name only those who have had the most lasting influence on my understanding of the system), not only would this book have been impossible to imagine, but the energies and the wisdom that it seeks to unbind and to make available to others would be unavailable and impenetrable to me, and not only my understanding but my life, too, would be incalculably poorer for that.

Why an American Book of Changes?

Over the past several decades, English translations of the ancient Chinese divination system known as the *I Ching*, or *Book of Changes*, have proliferated. The old verses, commentaries and concordances weave a rich brocade of meanings derived, sensibly enough, from close observation of the workings of the natural world and also from careful study of the habits of people and other animals. From such observations, the originators and early students of the system distilled a set of principles whose relevance to human activity has proven both universal and comprehensive. Unfortunately, they are far from universally comprehended.

The vast majority of people I meet who have encountered the *I Ching* report that they do not understand it, that its metaphysics is beyond them. Most seem convinced of its wisdom and efficacy, but they can't make heads or tails of its advice and don't know how to apply it. I'm quite sure that the underlying principles of the *I Ching*, while often subtle and mysterious, can be grasped by anyone sincere enough to make the attempt. But for the new reader (who often hasn't a clue about ancient Chinese customs, artifacts, history, poetry, symbolism, idiom and metaphor) the processes of deciphering, assimilating and applying the advice of a hexagram or a line of change to their particular problem or situation is bewildering and often intimidating.

When a set of ideas comes dressed in metaphors so layered, so foreign and so antiquated that they obscure what they ought to reveal, it is time for those ideas to change clothes. *The American Book of Changes* is a re-interpretation, not a new translation, of the sixty-four hexagrams and three hundred and eighty-four lines of the *I Ching*. It is written, not surprisingly, for Americans. Most English-speaking Westerners will be able to read and understand it easily enough, although they might not relate to it as readily as a Californian, a North Dakotan or a Floridian. It would be lovely to see, in my lifetime, the publication of a Brazilian Book of Changes, a Nigerian Book of Changes, a Lithuanian Book of Changes, and so on. While my purpose is, in part, to encourage a global diversification of the *I Ching*, I can only raise my own voice in my own North American dialect, using bits and pieces of the history, myth and metaphor of my own time and place, where few of us have much, if any, practical experience in fording rivers, much less in taking concubines or offering human and animal sacrifices to the ancestors.

The misogynistic paternalism of ancient China, having embedded itself in the verbiage of certain hexagrams, has posed a significant additional sticking point, for some readers, to the understanding and acceptance of the insights that the *I Ching* has to offer. If, for removing the occasion for such misunderstanding, I am accused of mere political correctness, then so be it. I have no apology to make. In my view, to dishonor the biologically female is to misunderstand the most fundamental principle of the *I Ching*, namely that the masculine and feminine energies are equal and indispensible to one another. I will go a step further in pointing out that the diversification and proliferation of gender identities and roles that have come to the surface in our own society over the past few decades is also in keeping with the idea that the essential energies of the male and female are infinitely inter-permeable and productive of a great variety of expressions.

I have included metaphors and symbols taken from aboriginal and other homegrown traditions as well as imported ones that have been assimilated and Americanized over the past few centuries. The result is a system of imageries and allusions as cobbled together as our society, one that struggles toward and strains against its own sense of unity and identity. *The American Book of Changes* is intended to serve those who want to make wiser choices and to develop, along the way, a less perturbable sense of personal integrity—one that is steeped in curiosity, adaptability and creativity.

Lines, Trigrams and Hexagrams

I have preserved the shorthand code words *yin* and *yang*, for the sake of their compactness. While they most certainly do sometimes imply the female and male sexes, respectively, they are not limited to distinctions based on sex. It is helpful, first, to speak of them separately, as wholly distinct packets of energy with opposing and complementary charges. (I use the word "charges" here in both the electromagnetic sense of positive versus negative and in the sense of duties, responsibilities, or jurisdictions—but only with the understanding that an individual of either sex may carry a charge of either kind, or of both, in any given situation.) *Yin* refers to the divine feminine as well as to the mundane, to the maternal, the physical, to matter, darkness, mystery, gestation and so on. Conversely, *yang* refers to the divine masculine and to the abstract, the paternal, the active, to energy, light, clarity, generative power and so on. Both lists could go on and on almost indefinitely, and the items listed might be parsed in a variety of ways, depending on the parser and the language in which the lists are made. (English long ago abandoned its gender-specificity, though we still cling to a few remnants such as the use of the feminine pronoun "she" to refer to ships and other vessels.)

Rather than laboring over which items to toss in the yin bin and which in the yang, the point is to recognize the remarkable ability of digital systems to represent the various states of energy and matter. Just as a certain string of ones and zeroes might represent a hexadecimal number such as #6ad289 (expressed as a specific tint of bluish green on a computer screen) the great variety of shadings found in the 384 lines of the 64 hexagrams of the *I Ching* are all derived from the two charged states: yin, represented by a dashed line,

and yang, represented by a solid line.

As Einstein's famous equation demonstrates, energy and matter are two expressions of a single underlying equivalence and, under the right conditions, either one can change into the other. This idea of equivalence means that yin is sometimes converted into yang, and vice versa. In a hexagram, a yin line that has become "extreme" (or has begun the process of changing into its opposite) is represented by two crossed lines:

while an extreme yang line is represented by a single continuous line in the form of a circle:

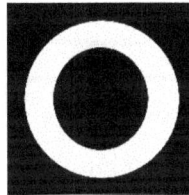

Lines can be paired to suggest a limited range of predominances, giving results like the following:

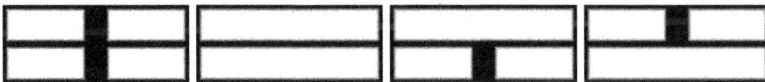

If we assign a negative charge to a yin line and a positive charge to a yang line, we might interpret such pairings to mean definitely no, definitely yes, maybe yes and maybe no, respectively. But this is probably less helpful than a simple yes/no response, which explains why, when the initial flip of a coin goes against us, we call for best two out of three, why there are seven games in the World Series, nine justices on the Supreme Court, and so on.

When lines appear in triplets, things get more decisive and more interesting. The eight possible arrangements of three yin and/or yang lines are called trigrams. Each trigram is associated with one or more natural elements or energies and carries additional meanings and associations as well, depending on its context.

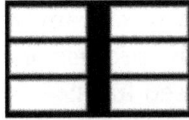

Earth: femininity, the center, groundedness, adaptability, the great mother, the womb, the color gold or yellow.

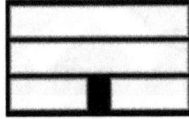

Penetration: the eldest daughter, learning, wood, wind, the color green.

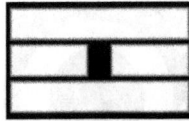

Lucidity: the middle daughter, reason, clarity, fire, the color red.

Joy: the youngest daughter, exuberance, gaiety, metal, a lake, the color silver or gray.

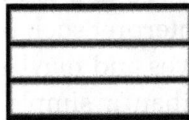

Sky: the father, outwardness, expansion, initiative, liberality, the color blue.

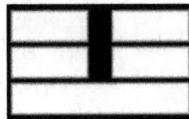

Emergence: the eldest son, shock, excitation, thunder, electricity, the color red-orange.

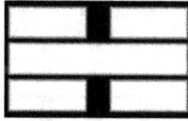

Danger: the middle son, confinement, crisis, a river gorge, the color black.

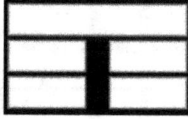

Stillness: the youngest son, inwardness, meditation, a mountain or stone, pale blue.

Finally, when any two trigrams are paired, the result will be one of the 64 hexagrams that form the basic structure of the *Book of Changes*:

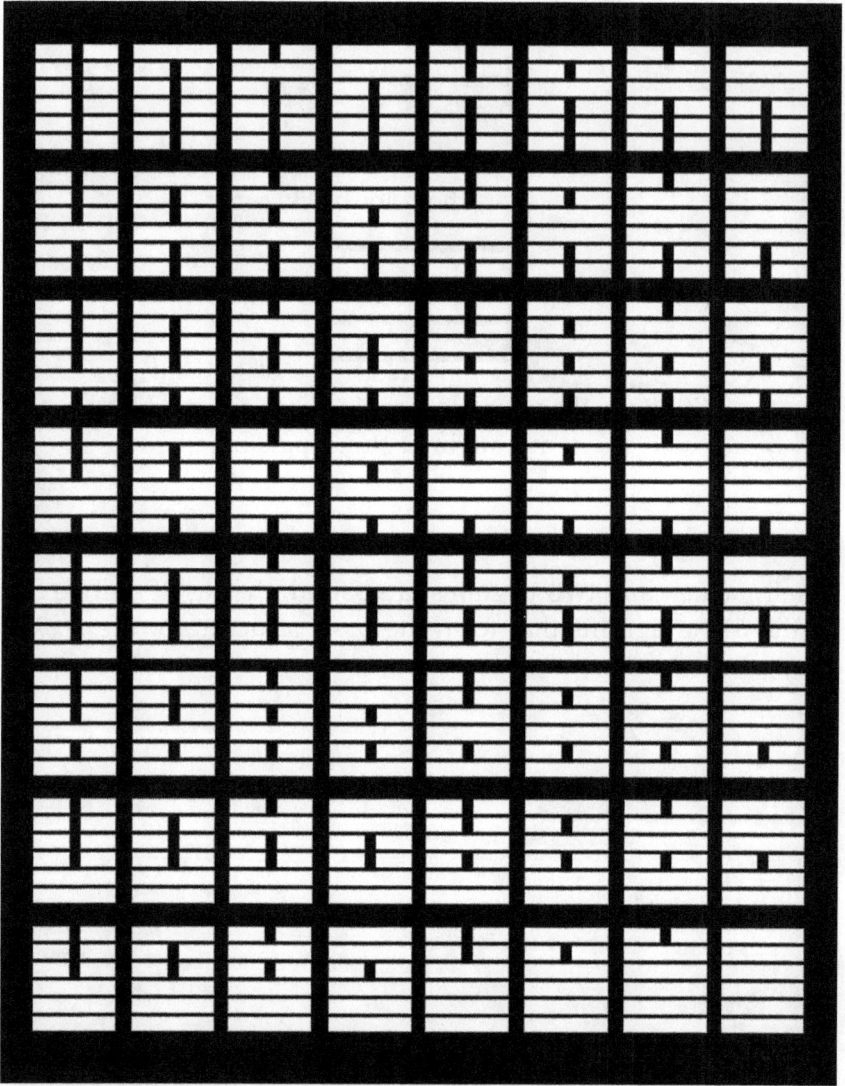

Yarrow Sticks, Coins and Dice

There are several ways to consult *The Book of Changes*, including a variety of online randomization applications that generate a hexagram at the click of a mouse. Many people, myself included, prefer the tactility of physical objects. The earliest consulting method used an assortment of yarrow sticks and a system for counting them. The physical method most often used today is to toss three coins together, six times, to generate the six lines of a hexagram. I would like to introduce a third method, which I have been using for many years more or less exclusively. This method employs a set of six dice (or, in a pinch, a single die tossed six times.) Standard playing dice work perfectly well.

The six dice are rolled one at a time and arranged from bottom to top, with the first die occupying the bottom position. An even number of dots represents a broken (yin) line (- -), and an odd number represents a solid (yang) line ($-$). Changing lines are indicated by ones (extreme yang) and sixes (extreme yin). In written notations, a one is represented by an unbroken circle (o) and a six by two crossed lines (x).

For my own use, I have created a set of dice with broken lines to replace the two and four (which I have placed on opposing rather than adjacent faces), two solid lines in place of the three and five (also on opposing faces), a circle in place of the one and an x in place of the six. If you'd like to make your own set of dice, a demonstration of the techniques for making a set using polymer clay might prove helpful. My instructions can be found at http:theamericaniching.com/dicedemo. Any durable material can be used to make dice, of course, including ceramic, wood, stone, bone, horn or antler. My polymer dice have withstood more than a decade of avid use and will probably serve for many years to come. They make a hexagram and any changing lines immediately visible, and unlike a standard set of dice, with odd and even numbers (1/6, 2/5, 3/4) on opposing faces, the new arrangement allows you to flip the entire stack over to reveal the 2nd hexagram.

An advantage that dice (either standard playing dice or the customized version) offer over coins and yarrow sticks is that an entire hexagram may be rolled without having to pause and mark down each line. Thus a hexagram is built more quickly and more fluidly, allowing for greater ease in maintaining concentration on the question or matter at hand. A 180° rotation of those dice that indicate changing lines (ones to sixes and vice versa) will yield the second hexagram, indicating the situation to come, after any changes have taken place. The same procedure could be followed using coins, of course, but you would need eighteen coins (three for each line) to do the work of six dice.

The odds that the roll of a die will result in a one or a six is somewhat greater than the odds that the coin toss method will yield a line of change: one in three as opposed to one in four. I find this increase to be an apt reflection of the accelerated pace of change that we face in the 21st Century. When change comes at us more rapidly, we have more to attend to, less time in which to craft an effective response, and a correspondingly greater need to inhibit the tendency to react reflexively.

Regardless of the means by which a hexagram is built, it will be built from the bottom up, so that the first line always refers to the bottom, and the sixth line always refers to the top. Once you have counted out your yarrow sticks, tossed your coins or rolled your dice, look at the first three lines to determine the lower trigram. Find that trigram in the vertical column to the left of the grid on the opposite page (also shown at the back of the book for easy reference). Then determine the upper trigram and find it in the horizontal row at the top of the grid. Follow the row in which you find the lower trigram until it intersects with the column of the upper trigram, and you will have your hexagram.

Find the hexagram by its number in the Table of Contents, and read the information pertaining to the hexagram as a whole, which includes the **associated concepts, images and attributes** and a description of the interaction of **the trigrams** as well as a description of the general meaning, energy or atmosphere and advice associated with the hexagram as a whole.

HEXAGRAM LOCATOR

2	23	8	20	16	35	45	12
15	52	39	53	62	56	31	33
7	4	29	59	40	64	47	6
46	18	48	57	32	50	28	44
24	27	3	42	51	21	17	25
36	22	63	37	55	30	49	13
19	41	60	61	54	38	58	10
11	26	5	9	34	14	43	1

If there are any changing lines, either extreme yin or extreme yang, read the text for the line or lines indicated (all ones and sixes on a standard set of dice, Xs and Os on customized dice). This will give a much more specific idea of the potential outcome of a situation or the likely result of a contemplated action. In some cases, the lines may seem to support or amplify one another; at other times, they may appear to contradict one another. In the latter case, several potential outcomes may co-exist. The situation may be highly volatile, for example, and timing could play a role. It will sometimes happen that a single outcome may be interpreted in more than one way or have several ramifications, all of which need to be taken into consideration.

When you have considered the advice of the hexagram as a whole and of each of the changing lines, you may turn to the second hexagram—the one that results from the changing lines turning into their opposites. Find the resulting hexagram in the same way, using the Hexagram Locator. Read only the overview provided for the second hexagram as a whole, disregarding the advice of the individual lines. The second hexagram offers insight into the condition that is most likely to prevail once the current situation has been resolved in the manner indicated in the first hexagram, along the specific lines of change indicated there. The second hexagram suggests a longer-term forecast—a result of the result, if you will, of the situation or action under consideration.

How to Formulate a Question

While there is no right or wrong way to consult the *Book of Changes*, certain approaches are more conducive to gaining useful information than others. The hexagrams are not, for the most part, designed to dictate behavior or to provide yes/no, right/wrong or true/false answers. Rather, they provide insights into the nature of a dilemma and the forces that are brought to bear upon it. The most important such forces to consider are those which are under the direct control or management of the one asking for guidance. For that reason, the most productive kind of question will often be of an open-ended or "what if" variety. For example, one might ask, "What is likely to happen if I take on the task of [___]?" or "What if I accept the offer of [___]?" or "What if I respond to [situation x] by doing [y]?" When the options available are unlimited or unclear, or when no potential solution presents itself, one might frame a question such as, "What is the best approach to take to [situation x]?"

Asking the same question more than once is not recommended as it will usually only serve to muddy the waters; however, if you are in fact looking for the answer to an up/down kind of question, it can be helpful to pose a question both negatively and positively and to compare the results. For example, if I want to decide whether to accept a particular invitation, I might ask, "What is the likely result of accepting?" and then "What is the likely result of declining?" In some cases, the advantages of one or the other course of action will be clear; in others, I may have to compare, contrast and choose. This method may be applied to multiple-choice questions as well, by tossing the dice as many times as there are options available.

It sometimes happens that a hexagram will answer an unasked, or masked, question. In the previous example, by asking, "What is the result of accepting invitation x?" I may in fact be wondering whether the invitation was sincere, I may feel an obligation but no real desire to accept, or it may be that the invitation represents something that I truly want or need but that might be better fulfilled in another way. The hexagrams sometimes seem to know us better than we know ourselves. In fact, a willingness to inquire might be the key required to unlock a cabinet in which one has stowed a secret ambition or an unsightly fear. The *Book of Changes* then becomes not only a method by which to decide what to do or not do but also a tool for self-examination and personal development. The more we delve into the concerns of daily life, the more we engage in self-discovery and the finer we draw the lines between practical, psychological, philosophical and spiritual concerns.

What Is Divination and How Does It Work?

I do not pretend to understand how or why the hexagrams of the *Book of Changes* manage to "read" our intentions (or energy states, if you prefer) but I will offer three untested hypotheses, each grounded in its own logic. I will begin with what I believe to be (as a stand-alone hypothesis, at least) the weakest of the three.

1. The Unseen Hand

The older I get (and the more I learn about physics) the less I am willing to dismiss as impossible. I cannot leave out of account the possibility that an unseen hand is involved in the tossing of coins, the selecting of a number of yarrow sticks or the rolling of dice in order to access a particular hexagram and its associated interpretation and advice. By "unseen hand" I mean any one of several, rather mystical entities. If one accepts or is willing to entertain, at least, the notion that a set of beliefs or ideas can attract the energy of spiritual beings (call them gods, departed souls, angels, higher selves or powers or what you will), then it is possible that such energies might direct the movements of physical objects in response to a sincere request for guidance. That I am not willing to dismiss this possibility does not mean that I regard it as the most likely; it simply means that it is as difficult to disprove as it is to prove. Nor do I believe that such unseen influences would need to operate in a way that excludes another explanation for which we might find relatively more evidence.

2. Unconscious Manipulation

The fine motor control of the arms, hands and fingers can produce movements of astonishing subtlety. A talented musician can evoke a stunning range and specificity of emotion by exerting control over the tension and drag of a strand of horse hairs over a set of fine steel strings. We may call the performance of a cellist "magical" without meaning that it literally invokes an occult influence or suggesting that the physical equipment has been tampered with in order to produce illusions like those of a stage magician. The physical apparatus of tendons, muscles, bones, brain and nerve fibers are the same as those used in flipping coins or rolling dice. The music we hear from the violinist is a result of extensive conscious training; the roll of a die we mark up to chance, but it is possible that the influence of the mind is powerful enough, at a pre-conscious level, to calculate the angle and force of a toss and so to influence the result.

3. The Mind as Organizer of Chaos and Manufacturer of Meaning

Finally, the human mind—in particular, those regions of the brain associated with the manufacture and interpretation of language— is a dedicated maker and manager of meaning. We can and do regularly—no, make that incessantly and vigorously—organize multiple torrents of information, suppressing and amplifying an astonishing variety of currents in such a way as to create a highly coordinated and interpretable world of objects and events that support and reinforce a sensitive and idiosyncratic set of assumptions, beliefs and operations that make each of us who we are. Our intentional and interpretive filters might well apply to any configuration of lines and associated texts, in response to a highly focused question, the kind of meaning we need to generate in a given moment. The sixty-four hexagrams provide, then, a lattice upon which to hang a new instance of meaning-making.

A Bonus Hypothesis: All of the Above

The likeliest scenario, to my mind (since I am no purist), is that these three possible explanations for the working of the hexagrams of the *Book of Changes* are mutually non-exclusive. I would suggest that there is no line of demarcation between the human hand and the world of the spirit, not the slightest gulf between the collective unconscious and a coordinated management of meaning, that the mind and body ought to be regarded as rather more of a continuum than a duality and that the worlds of the mind, body and spirit are interpenetrable in ways that are neither less nor more mystical than the bending of light rays through the lenses of a telescope, causing them to strike the retina in such a way as to allow us to resolve a distant image and to see it as if it were much closer to the eye. The science fiction writer Arthur C. Clarke stated as his third law of prediction that "any sufficiently advanced technology is indistinguishable from magic." I invite you to consider whether such advances in technology necessarily belong exclusively to the future. They may well have accompanied us out of the mists of prehistory.

1

The Eagle

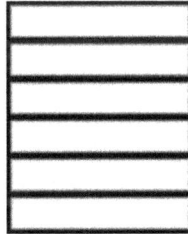

*The eagle, far-seeing, fierce,
and as independent in his
tastes as he is in his
attitude, presides over the sky.
With the stretch of his wings
he indicates the limits of
imagination.*

Associated concepts, images and attributes: The sky, heaven, flight, imagination, creativity, generative force, energy, activity, strength, majesty, independence, masculinity, spiritual guidance, the muse, ceaselessness, tirelessness, the competitive drive.

The Trigrams: Sky Repeated suggests the infinite

breadth, depth and height of the creative faculties.

You are imbued with, or need to channel, a soaring, can-do attitude and a keen sense of possibility. The situation is full of opportunity for creative expression, or ripe for a creative solution. Let your adventurous nature unfold and carry you with it. Remain playfully competitive. Spread your wings and ride the current of your imagination and independence.

Changing Lines

Change in the first line: Confined to the nest, the eaglet requires nourishment and protection. It is not time yet to take flight.

Your ideas need time to develop. Now is a time of creative mulling. There is great potential in the situation, but for the time being, that power remains latent. Keep things under wraps. Think and act in terms of brooding, nurturing and protecting. Don't rush to act. A creative brainchild is still in its infancy. Exposing it to outside influences at this stage will inhibit its development and invite disaster.

Change in the second line: The fledgling takes flight.

The time has come to test a new idea or to enter a new field of activity. Experiment boldly, but don't forget to ask for advice from those more experienced than you. You begin to feel your own power and self-reliance as well as the uplifting currents of energy that support you.

Change in the third line: The sky-hunter is on the wing, keeping a sharp eye, flying fast and far from sunup to sundown.

Remain ceaselessly active and vigilant now. There is no stopping and no turning back. Pursue your goals with singleness of purpose and diligent attention to detail. Burn the midnight oil.

Change in the fourth line: Diving and swooping. The wind is his playground.

Maintaining a spirit of adventure and playfulness will keep you fresh. If you keep circling higher and higher, you risk losing your touch, your youthful energy and your competitive edge. Remember that the game you play, no matter the stakes, is still a game.

Change in the fifth line: At the height of his power, the eagle stretches and soars.

You are at the top of your game. There is room for expansion, generosity and greatness. Get in touch with your own deepest levels of joy and with that which is great in you, and stay in touch with wise counsel. Be great of heart.

Change in the top line: The eagle is brought down from his nest in the stars. Beware!

Heed the warning and desist! You overreach yourself. You have become like the arrogant young Icarus with his wings of wax, who flew too close to the sun. The way to avoid his fate is to remember that you are a hunter. The nourishment that sustains you is not in the heavens but on earth.

If all the lines are changing:

Eagles flying together, none leading, none following.

At its fullest and noblest expression, creative power resides in egoless confidence. You fly with the spirit of the times.

2

The Buffalo

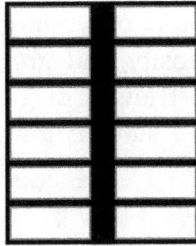

The buffalo is sturdy. She provides for
herself, for her young, and for the people
of the earth. Without her there is no
shelter, no home, no center. Without a
center, there is no direction.

Associated concepts, images and attributes: Maternal power, the earth, matter, concrete form, the body, nurturing, acceptance, tolerance, domesticity, routine, the home.

The Trigrams: Earth Repeated gives rise to an image of the Great Plains of North America and of the vast herds of bison indigenous to the continent.

The second hexagram speaks of a lasting maternal influence, especially in terms of the provision of care and devotion, with an emphasis on the physical body, the material world, and sacred traditions. Borrowing from the Lakota tradition, this influence is expressed in terms of the legend of White Buffalo Woman. She reminded the women of the tribe that the work of their hands and the fruit of their bodies kept the people alive. "You come from the Mother, from the Earth," she said. "What you do is as great as anything warriors do." She also gave them the sacred pipe, the one holy object in the making of which both men and women take part. Men carve the bowl and make the stem; women decorate it with bands of colored porcupine quills. When a couple marries, they both hold the pipe, while a red cloth is wound around their hands, binding them together as one.

Another key feature of native spiritual outlooks is found in the powers ascribed to the Four Directions, which occur either literally or in symbolic form throughout the stories of the Lakota. Often represented by particular colors or animals, the Four Directions come into balance in order to heal the world. The central point of balance signifies a fifth direction. Four brothers represent East, West, North and South. Their sister, White Buffalo Woman, occupies the center.

The principle of receptivity stands not in opposition to, but in a complementary relationship with, that of creativity. The two are no more separable than time and space, energy and matter, the masculine and the feminine, the rational and the intuitive, performance and audience. (The list of such pairings is virtually inexhaustible.) The positive is inherent in the negative, and vice versa, whether or not it finds expression in a given moment. Like the two sides of a coin, this duality is regarded as an eternal condition that is universally applicable to all things and in all situations.

The situation illustrated here requires patience, reserve and receptivity. The quiet strength embodied in the second hexagram of the Book of Changes requires and facilitates the coalescence of energy rather than its release, domesticity rather than adventurism, pre-conscious brooding rather than the implementation of the creative mental faculties. The conscious activity recommended for the time being is that of the mundane, repetitive and meditative sort. Enormous strength and fertility makes itself available to you, but the accumulation of power—not its expression—is important now. Pay attention to detail and to subtle information. Ruminate, support, gestate, nurture.

Changing Lines

Change in the first line: The ground is white with frost. The buffalo's coat grows thick with the approach of winter.

This indicates a time of withdrawal and solidification that might make itself felt in a tendency toward rigidity. Pay attention to the subtle signs of the time and take appropriate measures. Prepare, as it were, for a hard winter by making certain of your own stores of warmth and nourishment, not for the sake of selfishly hoarding them but in order to care for those around you as well as yourself.

Consider carefully whether the course of action you are considering is itself a sign of withdrawal and distrust, in which case it may be unwise to pursue it. Migrate, if you can, to a warmer climate of the soul or way of thinking.

Change in the second line: The buffalo stands on four legs, for the four ages of humankind. She represents the universe and distributes her energy to the four cardinal directions. By virtue of her existence and her fertility, the people are provided for.

You find yourself in the quiet center of things. The situation is pregnant with possibility. This is exactly as it should be; don't worry. The signs are favorable, and there is no need to make a plan. Move with the changes just as a pregnant cow moves when the herd moves, by instinct rather than deliberation. You are in the right position to meet any need or crisis that arises.

Change in the third line: The herd follows its accustomed pattern of migration, closing its ranks as it moves. In this way, one's worth is contained and concealed, yet effectiveness is released.

The advice given here is to accept the power of conventional ways of doing things, to work within a system, perhaps, or to remain behind the scenes. This is not to be misconstrued as a way of avoiding responsibility, but by keeping your head down and by focusing on the tasks at hand while keeping your long-range goals firmly in mind, you can make yourself far more effective than by taking the initiative in a more brash or noticeable way.

Change in the fourth line: She wears a poker face and carries her purpose bundled in a bag. There is neither blame nor praise to be found.

There is no indication of a good outcome or of a poor one. You hold your cards close to the chest, but so does your opponent. You may be looking for answers where none are to be found, for approval or approbation that is not forthcoming. The point here is that what you seek, you already have.

Change in the fifth line: There is gold in the earth. Miners come with their pans and picks and shovels.

Just as the gold bound up in the seams of a mountain can sometimes be found in a stream bed, so your true worth, when it reveals itself of its own accord, will be sought out by those who value it. This can be a confusing time of claims and counter-claims, and you must decide what it is that you value in yourself as well as in others. When you know that, you will attract those who understand and appreciate your true worth. This separates the gold from the sand, as it were, and leads to still greater and truer valuation of the self and of what matters to you.

Change in the top line: The eagles clasp talons. Their blood is spilled; its colors are red and white and blue. The herd is decimated, only the tongues taken, while the rest stinks to the heavens.

Violence is indicated, like that of a civil war or a program of genocide. The action contemplated is extreme and will provoke a conflict in which both sides inflict such damages that victory becomes worse than meaningless. It is better to stop your advance than to indulge in arrogant behavior that threatens to destroy something of real value to your own nature and to the sustainability of life.

If all the lines are changing:

Your way of life endures. When you achieve sustainability of purpose like this, ideas of progress and regress are rendered meaningless. As the slogan goes, you become the change you want to see in the world, and in fact, that change means real stability.

3

Birth

```
▬▬▬ ▬▬▬
▬▬▬▬▬▬▬
▬▬▬ ▬▬▬
▬▬▬▬▬▬▬
▬▬▬ ▬▬▬
▬▬▬ ▬▬▬
```

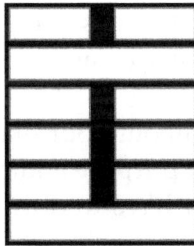

The earth shudders, and the sky opens.
Her water breaks amid cries of wonder
and alarm.

Associated concepts, images and attributes: Emergence and emergency, the birth of a new idea, chaos, a brainchild, a difficult labor, uncertain beginnings, risk.

The Trigrams: Quake and Water give rise to the image of the spasms of childbirth and the breaking of the amniotic sac, signifying upheaval, danger and the uncertainty of a new beginning.

The excitement and chaos of the new emerges. A sense of urgency must be channeled effectively, the challenges of a new situation handled with dedication, strength and gentleness. Devote your energy to the massing resources and to putting things in order, corralling divergent aims in order to create a unified vision and sense of purpose. It is important to clearly define your mission and to set relevant goals. A profusion of interests, however, makes it unwise to impose strict discipline at this time or to attempt to gain adherence to your own view of things prematurely. When anything at all is possible, it is important to balance listening and directing. Allowing things to take their own course will lead to a dissipation of energies, but trying to rule the situation with too firm a hand only incites rebellion. Your challenge is to marshal your own resources while respecting competing agendas.

Changing Lines

Change in the first line: When the newborn emerges from the womb, the first order of business is to announce an agenda — namely, to bond with the mother and find the breast.

It is important to be clear about your plans and to anchor them to your own deepest sense of purpose and connectedness. What does this new matter or project have to do with your core values and with the place you wish to occupy in the world? How does it sustain you? Once you have defined your mission in terms of its relevance to you personally, be quick to announce your intentions to those who may be affected by them, especially those in a position to provide the support and encouragement you need. Keeping secrets from your most intimate circles will not serve you. Sharing your central purpose invites an exchange of ideas and establishes a network for the sharing of resources.

Change in the second line: Giving birth to a prickly pear.

Why do you adopt such a defensive attitude with potential supporters? First you reach out to them, then you bristle and turn away, keeping them at a distance. A connection is available to you that seeks to help, not hinder. If you can drop the hostilities on your end, even though it may still be a while before a damaged or neglected relationship bears fruit, you can trust that it will turn out well in the end.

Change in the third line: Chasing butterflies without a net, the child toddles into a dark wood.

You are chasing one lovely idea after another and getting lost in a forest of possibilities. Stop now, return to your base of operations and try to remember what's truly important to the long-term growth and sustainability of your plans. An honest admission of inexperience is the first step in gaining experience. If you need help staying focused, don't allow pride to deter you from seeking it out.

Change in the fourth line: Pass out the cigars!

Like a difficult birth, the troubled launch of a creative idea or project has turned out well. Adopt the stance of a new parent taking a child in your arms for the first time. Forge an irreversible bond. Take on a permanent commitment to the new and demanding element in your life. It doesn't mean that your troubles are over; quite the opposite, in fact. Nevertheless, this is certainly a moment worth celebrating, not only for you but for everyone involved. Pledge your allegiance and embrace your new role in front of the whole community.

Change in the fifth line: Counting the fingers and toes of the youngest child. The eldest is not yet grown.

You have found a way to provide for the future through the principle of redundancy. Make certain that the details are in order, and everything will go well. While this is not the time to launch a grand new enterprise, it serves you well to repeat the success of your initial efforts and to enjoy the cumulative benefits. Provide support for those upon whom the future depends and remain adaptable to new developments.

Change in the top line: Miscarriage: not a beginning but an end of possibilities.

This is not a productive way to set out. A premature presumption of power invites disaster. It will bleed you of personal energy and material resources. This is not something you can simply "manage" or fix. It spells the end of your plans. If you do not abandon this strategy, you may have to abandon the entire project. If it is already too late, grieve the loss and move on.

4

The Spring

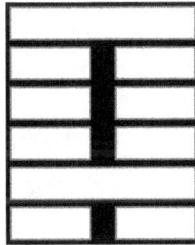

The young mind is fluid and expansive,
curious in every direction at once.
Because it is, in fact, impossible to learn
from the experience of others, the
responsibility of the teacher is to provide
experiences wisely, safely and with as
little interference as possible.

Associated concepts, images and attributes: Wisdom, the
beginner mind, youthful ignorance, learning, a parent-child or
student-teacher relationship, cultivation of new talent, mentoring,
initiation, the end of innocence, good vs. evil, forbidden
knowledge, taboo, risk, recklessness, foolishness, inexperience.

The Trigrams: Water and Mountain give rise to the image of a spring gushing forth at the foot of a mountain, signifying the sharing of accumulated knowledge and wisdom through the conduit of relationship between the wise sage (here represented as reserved in speech and not easily disturbed by external circumstances) and the innocent youth (experimental, adaptable and far more likely to babble). In certain of the lines, the image of an apple is invoked as a symbol of education.

Because preconception clouds the mind and limits perception, the wisest approach to a difficult or frustrating problem is to set aside presumption, to forget what we already "know" about the situation confronting us. While this may be easier said than done, the fourth hexagram offers suggestions for reducing the stress that precludes learning and for striking a balance between seriousness of purpose and the requisite sense of play that serves as the foundation for all learning.

You are invited to explore the process of maturation, to encourage growth and the acquisition of knowledge and experience. The situation involves a relationship – either internal or external – like that between a wise teacher and a naive pupil. Experimentation is encouraged, but within a protected or secluded, school-like environment.

The situation is fluid. Because it is not yet fully developed, it must be handled with care and close attention. The seeker may not be prepared to undertake anything of great consequence and may feel a certain hunger for knowledge; however, relevant information will not be acquired through asking the same question again and again and hoping for a different answer nor by blindly adopting authoritative opinions. The best remedy for inexperience is to make mistakes that can be corrected and refined.

You are encouraged to take a leap, to make a mess, to break some eggs! Whatever it is you want to do, be willing to do it poorly at first. You need feedback that only the rough and tumble of playful experience can provide.

Lines of Change

Change in the first line: The arrow has missed the apple. Correct your aim and try again. William Tell learned in the same way.

A first attempt brings no results, or worse than none, but the great thing about being human is that you have the ability to learn from your mistakes. If you keep doing the same thing without making adjustments, or if you pretend that you've actually accomplished something when you haven't, you'll end up looking and feeling not only foolish but dangerous, with nothing to show for your efforts. Don't just try, try again. First, analyze the failure, then try something different. If you find something that works, refine it through repetition. Practice the successful completion of a necessary task again and again in a safe or low-risk environment, until success becomes second nature and you can perform with confidence regardless of the circumstances.

Change in the second line: Capable of establishing a home and taking on parenthood.

A level of maturity has been achieved, enabling the one who has been cared for to, in turn, take on the task of caring for and educating others, to establish a home and a way of life. The energy of the situation is like that of a young person entering into a marriage or a position of authority and responsibility. Step up to the task; assume the new role.

Change in the third line: The gunslinger's wife is the apple of the young cowboy's eye. This will not end well.

It is unwise to regard as an educational opportunity the kind of mistake that you know in advance is a mistake. You are tempted by something attractive that does not belong to you. If you persist, there will be consequences that you are ill-equipped to handle. Let the opportunity pass.

Change in the fourth line: Solitary confinement in an ivory tower.

The idea of seclusion for the sake of learning can be taken too far. You have isolated yourself from what is real. It distorts your view of life and renders your work not only inaccessible but irrelevant and unhelpful. It would be far better to expose yourself and your ideas to the rough and tumble of a more competitive environment.

Change in the fifth line: The beginner's mind is open.

Acceptance of one's own ignorance is the first step on the journey to experience and must accompany every step along the path of wisdom. Choosing such a path opens one to an infinite set of possibilities.

Change in the sixth line: A brick in the wall.

Punishing ignorance does not accomplish the task of educating inexperience; it only creates resentment. Abuse, including self-abuse, is not excused by a failure to understand a problem. The remedy for a lack of insight is to empower the mind, not beat it into submission.

5

The Lull

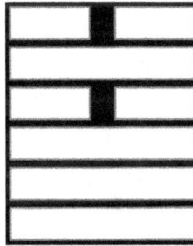

The sky broods in a most cumulative
manner. When it hatches a plan, it's
wise to be caught aware.

Associated concepts, images and attributes: Patience, timing, attentiveness, waiting on (serving) and waiting for, anticipating, abiding, relaxed alertness, delayed gratification; conversely: hesitation, anxiety, exposure to risk.

The Trigrams: Sky and Water suggest an approaching storm that offers both nourishing rain and the possibility of danger.

An impending crisis keeps you on your toes. Because the situation has not yet matured, it is vital that you remain fully present and attentive to subtle signs and patterns, even if nothing important seems to be happening just yet. Tend to the needs of the situation as a good waiter tends to the needs of many patrons at once, keeping a sharp eye and a low profile until something is called for. Timing is everything. Make yourself useful during this period of uncertainty by attending to the details or ordinary life, but don't lose sight of the need to take immediate action if and when the storm hits.

Be calm and carry on. The situation could change at a moment's notice, or it could all blow over. Wait for the right moment to make a move.

Changing Lines

Change in the first line: At a distance, waiting.

You feel removed from the situation, perhaps disconnected from what's going on. Don't let this sense of alienation gain a foothold in your mind. You are right where you need to be for now, doing the right thing by waiting attentively. Your time will come, probably sooner than you think.

Change in the second line: Waiting and watching from the beach, pacing on the sand.

A sense of expectation and anxiety sets in. You are exposed to new influences that may or may not be reliable. It's difficult to gain traction, since nothing is certain. Conditions shift underfoot with every step you take. Everyone has an opinion, and in the face of uncertainty and boredom, the rumor mill can really get cranking. All the constant chatter — whether it comes from outside sources or just bounces around inside your own head — can prove highly distracting. Don't put your faith in everything you hear, read or imagine right now. Idle speculation is natural, but you don't have to get caught up in it. Keep your ears, eyes and mind open, because the situation is still developing.

Change in the third line: Camping in the mud while the storm clouds build.

The thing you care about is at risk. You are over-exposed and bogged down in details and conflicting interests that rob you of mobility and adaptability. Should the storm hit now, should you encounter difficulty or come under attack, you will find your position difficult to defend — particularly if you are entangled with or beholden to special interests or suspicious people. Think your situation over carefully while you still have time; do what it takes to extricate yourself while you can.

Change in the fourth line: For the soldier in a foxhole with a live grenade, the wait is over.

This is not the time to explore your options. The only thing to do is to get out. Now!

Change in the fifth line: Eating and drinking in good company. Waiting cheerfully.

You can afford to relax and enjoy the moment. Take a little time off. If there are problems, they'll be there when you come back to them, and you'll be able to approach them with renewed vigor and enthusiasm. For now, enjoy what you have in the way of comforts and easy friendships. Use this time to fortify yourself.

Change in the top line: Open the door and let them come in.

Outside influences arrive without an invitation. Receive them graciously nevertheless. Play the host. The situation is unusual, to say the least, but new information is available to you that you could not have anticipated. Hear this new thing out, but don't get sidetracked or talked into letting go of your own ideals.

6

Conflict

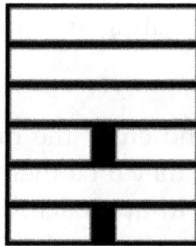

*The storm has broken. It is not wise to
let yourself become electrified.*

Associated concepts, images and attributes: Disagreement,
hostility, contentiousness, litigation. Conversely: negotiation,
conflict avoidance, conflict resolution.

The Trigrams: Water and Sky give rise to the image of a deluge,
signifying a time of open conflict and the steps needed in order to
mitigate damages.

There is a strong possibility of open conflict. Harsh words and
actions make themselves readily available. Conflict is sometimes
necessary in order to resolve tension, to set right an old wrong or
to defend something vital to your own well-being or to that of
someone who is dependent on you for protection. The general
advice given here is to stand up for yourself, not to be bullied or
intimidated, to champion a cause, to right a wrong, to oppose an

injustice. The situation will not improve if you let it slide; it will only embolden those who seek to take advantage of you.

Conflict has implications that go beyond the epic struggle of good versus evil, however. The goal is never polarization or victory for its own sake. In the physical world, friction provides traction. Just so in the social and political realms. Without differences of opinion, nothing changes for the better; artificial rigidity and formalism set in, resulting in stagnation and decay. The purpose of open debate is to reach, if not agreement in every particular, at least an airing of the matter in the hope of reaching a mutually amenable solution. Diplomacy lubricates the mechanism of argumentation, but honest debate is driven by passion on both sides. Friction, properly managed, moderates direction and acceleration and accomplishes real work.

Changing Lines

Change in the first line: Don't get drawn into a petty argument.

The matter is trivial, truly not worth your time and attention. If you don't perpetuate the conflict, it will pass of its own accord. Find something else to occupy your time.

Change in the second line: Life is too short to pick a losing battle.

An argument that you simply can't win will only deplete your resources. Retreat for now and associate with more like-minded people or turn your mind to more agreeable matters. Don't just back down and stand glaring at your enemy; that won't accomplish anything. Instead, go be of real service elsewhere.

Change in the third line: Battling demons, devouring wisdom.

You need practical and spiritual advice. You confront issues rooted in your own past, though they come clothed in the form of an outside adversary. Access the wisdom and power of an experienced negotiator, mentor or spiritual advisor who knows what you're up against and adopt that person's strength as your

21

own. Thus fortified, you can make a reasoned and determined argument. Don't back down from this one. Fight your way to a just conclusion. Keep pressing your advantage until the matter is resolved, but understand that in a time of out-and-out conflict, your social obligations may have to take a back seat. This matter requires your full time and attention.

Change in the fourth line: A tactical retreat.

Be honest with yourself; you can't win this battle under the prevailing conditions. If you hold back now and refuse to be drawn in, however, conditions will soon become more favorable. Be calm and wait for the right moment, when you can press your claim on your own terms, with greater self-assurance. If you engage in confrontation now, you will fail.

Change in the fifth line: The right judge hears your case.

Now is the time. State your case with clarity and conviction. You will get a favorable hearing. Not only will the situation that brought you to this point of conflict be resolved, the recognition you receive for effectively handling it will create an opportunity to forge a significant connection for the future.

Change in the top line: Winning at all costs, you will be stripped of your good name and your title.

You want to fight on to the bitter end, besting all comers and proving that you are the ultimate warrior. You may win recognition this way, but you'll get no peace. You'll be forced to defend yourself again and again, and in the end, you will lose everything, including your honor and your dignity. The glory you seek is illusory at best and certainly not worth the sleep you'll lose. Desist.

7

The Team

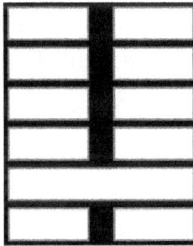

*Pulling a team together is like drawing
water out of the earth. You can't just
talk it up and tell it what to do; you have
to prime the well, pump the water to the
surface and, once it has decided to heed
your will, you still have to keep it
channeled. Otherwise, it goes right back
to what it was doing before you came
along.*

Associated concepts, images and attributes: Organization, discipline, esprit de corps, leadership, marshalling forces, event or project management, waging a campaign.

The Trigrams: Water and Earth give rise to the image of an aquifer, signifying vast resources that may be drawn upon in a time of need.

A well-organized team is necessary in order to carry out a great undertaking. The requisite skills of effective leadership include the ability to recognize individual talent and to harness the ambitions of others in the service of a common goal. Those loyal to a cause must be roused of their own volition to take on their separate tasks, to coordinate their efforts with other members of the team, to accept both the leadership of one who personally embodies their common aims and the yoke of discipline required for a specific purpose and for the duration of a specific project. Human resources must be treated with unwavering respect, guided by true leadership and inspired by a worthy goal.

The situation calls for a disciplined gathering and deployment of the resources at your disposal. Keep a watchful eye on the potential for laxity on the one hand and excessive zeal on the other.

Changing Lines

Change in the first line: Strict order and discipline are required before the game is played.

Enthusiasm often wanes at the first sign of difficulty. You need to understand and manage both expectations and accountability. At the same time, the regulations you institute must not so micro-manage the situation that you end up hamstringing your own efforts and impeding your power. Be inspiring, demand excellence of yourself and expect it of others.

Change in the second line: The place of the player-coach is in the middle of things.

You are in a position to assume active leadership of an effectively organized force. With that power comes a mandate to wield it, to take action personally and to inspire others through your own participation. The use of force in this instance is not a mistake, it is your duty. Engage with honor, courage and a sense of purpose. Exemplify excellence. The service you render now will affect the outcome of the current situation and alter the course of your life.

Change in the third line: At the start of a new game, the rookie tallies losses.

A fear of failure clings to you. Haunted by old mistakes, you go foredoomed to fulfill your own worst predictions. You risk exposing yourself to injury only to prove yourself right. This is no way to proceed. Your fear is inspired not by the current situation but by conditions that are no longer relevant. It is crucial that you shake off the past before you go on. Otherwise, you defeat yourself before you have a chance to succeed.

Change in the fourth line: The game is won. Take the knee. Let the clock run out.

You have made substantial progress, winning recognition and territory. As a force to be reckoned with, you are able to negotiate a favorable settlement that allows you to make the most of a period of rest. You have reached a new plateau or achieved a satisfactory goal. It is neither necessary nor beneficial to press on at this time. Relax and consolidate your gains. You won't be making a mistake.

Change in the fifth line: The ball is snapped. The blitz is on.

The situation is abundantly clear. It cannot be avoided, it is already upon you. You will have to improvise, and quickly. Scramble! Find a way to advance! If you panic and start giving ground now, you're done for.

Change in the top line: The season is over. A dynasty has been founded. Nevertheless, the work of rebuilding the franchise begins.

Order must be maintained during a period of recuperation and recalibration. Otherwise, everything you have worked so hard to accomplish will disintegrate around you. Any internal bickering and petty rivalries will have to be stamped out, while those who fall under your new jurisdiction must be welcomed with civility and fairness. It is vital that you find and employ only the best people for the work of restructuring or expanding an enterprise. The small-minded and self-important must be banished from positions of authority.

8

E Pluribus Unum

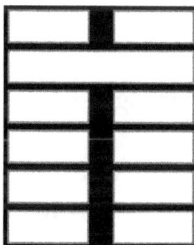

In color theory red and blue make purple, in politics they make mud.

Associated concepts, images and attributes: Union, unity of purpose, holding together, consolidation, amalgamation, adherence, commonality, the social fabric.

The Trigrams: Earth and Water give rise to the image of a vast inland sea or great lake, suggesting a pooling of resources, a community of interests and a collective spirit.

A single strong principle or element (suggested by the unbroken fifth line) holds several weaker elements together. The situation is one in which the qualities and attributes of a great variety of influences need to be taken into consideration. On a personal level, you are invited to assess your own circles of influence and association. Try to understand the essential nature of a relevant group and of each of its members and what they bring to the table. Decide with whom and what you actually belong.

Because so many points of view present themselves for consideration, there are many different ways to frame your question. It is right to continue with further consultation, pondering the matter thoroughly. It is important that you do this work now rather than later. Without a unified sense of purpose — a mission statement, if you will, to which all parties can willingly sign on — everything is subject to the whims of powerful individuals and to the passing moods of the group. You will then find yourself battered by opinions from all sides. Move to the center by aligning yourself with the highest possible common denominator. Only from such a standpoint is it possible to seek consensus.

Changing Lines

Change in the first line: Joining.

You have found a group that overflows with strong and loving support. You would do well to join with them. You will find even more support coming your way if you do.

Change in the second line: Your place is in the center of things.

You have formed a connection that places you at the center of your group, near the source of its energy and purpose. This is very fortunate. Treat this connection with respect. Don't let it slip through your fingers.

Change in the third line: You are hanging with the wrong crowd. Don't sign on.

These are not your people, and this is not the place for you. You have no deep connection to this idea or these influences. If you stick around, you will suffer injury and humiliation.

Change in the fourth line: On the outside, looking in.

Don't be discouraged. This particular group may have formed without you, and you may feel like an appendage rather than a true member, but such loose association has its benefits. You remain your own person, independent in thought and action. What's more, you have an opportunity, provided you stick to your guns and continue the valuable work that you are doing on your own, to exert a powerful and beneficial influence that moves the group in a positive direction.

Change in the fifth line: I see your true colors, shining through.

You seek connections and long to find your place in the social world. You won't get anywhere by trying to impress people, much less by trying to convert them to your way of thinking. Allow your true nature, your values, goals and sense of purpose to be seen. That is really all you need to do. You will find willing adherents who don't need to be persuaded. Be loyal to them. Let the others go their own way.

Change in the top line: Things fall apart. The center cannot hold.

There is no unifying principle to be found here, no valid sense of purpose and no leadership worth following. Leave. Don't even bother to make excuses. Just go.

9

Delayed Gratification

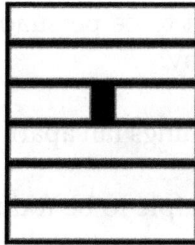

*The sky, inscribed by high winds and
clouds, leaves its message both
inscrutable and dry.*

Associated concepts, images and attributes: Due diligence, sustained effort, patience, expectation without apparent results, faith in the absence of evidence.

The Trigrams: Sky and Wind give rise to the image of passing clouds, signifying weather patterns that offer no immediate promise of rain.

While this may seem like a time of continual toil with little to show for your efforts, it is nevertheless an important stage in the development of your ideas. By paying attention to the myriad details that require your attention, you prepare inwardly for the future, when rewards will manifest outwardly. For now, maintain an attitude of diligence. Enjoy your work for its intrinsic value. Meet each need as it arises. Don't look for quick results. You can predict neither overnight profits nor overt signs of approval. Instead, settle into a rhythm of work that you can enjoy for its own sake, knowing that you're in it for the long haul.

Changing Lines

Change in the first line: Lost, you find your way again.

It's as if you've been fighting your way through a wilderness, relentlessly entangled in details and to-do lists, when suddenly, you come to a clearing and recognize where you are. You can get back on the path again.

Change in the second line: Hauled back to the path like a dog on a leash.

Lost, confused, disoriented and driven to distraction, events or people have conspired to intervene and force you back to the way you need to go. You can't take any credit for it, but accept your good fortune and get back to work with a renewed sense of purpose.

Change in the third line: Sitting in the ditch with a broken axle. Nobody's talking to each other.

You aren't moving forward, because something is broken. Rather than communicating about the problem and how to resolve it, you just want to blame someone. Sadly, nothing's going to get done that way. Ask for the help you need and lend whatever help you can.

Change in the fourth line: Pedal to the metal. Leave bad blood behind.

The disputes that hindered you have been settled. Let go of them and follow your renewed sense of inspiration and purpose. Act boldly now.

Change in the fifth line: Inspiration strikes. Share the electricity.

Because you are inspired, you have an opportunity to inspire others. Bind yourself to them and them to your purpose. Don't be afraid to make this connection. Use it to do good work and to bring the benefit to everyone involved.

Change in the top line: Fat drops of rain. The drought is broken.

An important goal is reached. The blessings fall like a refreshing rain. Invigorated, you and those around you are able to carry on. Enjoy this time. It doesn't mean that the hard work is over or that you should start taking on new projects. The fact that your burden momentarily feels a little lighter is no reason to add to it.

10

Conduct

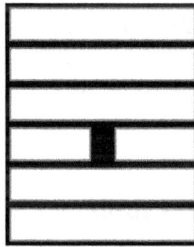

When metal touches power, sparks will
fly. Conduct yourself as if you carry an
extremely high voltage. Because you do.

Associated concepts, images and attributes: Correct behavior, cautious optimism, showing respect, the way of power.

The Trigrams: Lake and Sky suggest a playful and joyous mirroring of the powerful spirit of creation, like a child who emulates an elder.

Conduct is both an outward expression of personal integrity and a continual process of negotiation with the outside world. What is most important under the current circumstances is to negotiate wisely with those of greater power and experience than you. The balancing act you need to perform is that of following your own path to power while recognizing that the trail has been blazed by others who now stand in a position to assist you or impede you, because the path is steep. If you proceed too brusquely, without showing respect or following the necessary protocol, you can easily be struck down, even destroyed, with impunity.

If you follow people of true worth, you will have less of a problem. Model your behavior on theirs but without fawning. The only way to earn the approval of a person of merit is through merit. Show respect, not fear. Avoid arrogance at all costs. Be considerate of others regardless of their station, and you will be able to proceed with alert caution.

Changing Lines

Change in the first line: It's not complicated.

Be simple and direct in your dealings. No one can fault you for that.

Change in the second line: Climbing alone.

You are outside the social network for now. You don't need to attract attention, just go about your business and enjoy the freedom of movement you are afforded.

Change in the third line: Nothing behind your bluff.

Pretentious behavior puts you in danger. You act like a lone foot soldier who thinks he commands a battalion. Nobody else is fooled by your bravado. If you are specifically called upon to sacrifice yourself in this way, make sure that your cause is worthy of such selfless adherence to duty.

Change in the fourth line: Face time.

You come face to face with true power. Make the most of it. State your case with clarity and conviction. Practice the art of persuasion. Don't be intimidated. Step up to the plate.

Change in the fifth line: You have a choice to make. That choice is clear.

Part company with that which no longer serves your purpose. Its influence is detrimental to your cause, and you know it. It may have been harmful all along, but now that you see it for what it is, self-deception is a luxury you cannot afford. It's time to move along by doing the right thing.

Change in the top line: The pattern of your life emerges.

Pause to reflect on the course of events and the choices you've made that have brought you to your current position. You will begin to see a pattern emerge. You are connected to a deeper sense of purpose than mere personal ambition. It is this connection that opens doors for you. It has been with you from the beginning. It will continue to lead the way for as long as you remain available to follow.

11

Stability

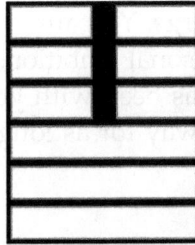

The wise hawk understands that power
preserves peace and is not afraid to use
it. The wise dove understands that peace
preserves power and is not afraid to keep
it.

Associated concepts, images and attributes: Peace, harmonious conditions, prosperity, progress, mutual support and recognition between the social and economic classes.

The Trigrams: Sky and Earth, each firmly occupying the position usually associated with the other, suggest a time of "heaven on earth" or a temporal condition of peace and prosperity.

Peace reigns in society or in the individual heart when the stronger elements voluntarily provide for the support of the weaker, who are in turn receptive to their influence. When this happens, the result is no mere trickling down of wealth, but an upwelling of prosperity and expansion, a flowering of culture that is firmly rooted in the stable conditions that give rise to it. It is important to make the most of such a time, since nothing, not even stability, can last forever.

The situation illustrated here can be likened to the form of government envisioned by the founding fathers of the United States, who distributed power among the executive, legislative and judicial institutions. They designed a system of checks and balances to reflect the will of the people while safeguarding against the erratic nature of populist whims. The long-term stability and prosperity of an organization or an individual is rooted in the ability to manage and adapt to changing conditions. Just as the viability of any complex organism depends on the exchange of individual cells, the life of the mind on the exchange and evolution of ideas, and the wellness of the heart on the give and take of affectionate support in times of joy and grief alike, so the cycle of birth, death and rebirth is essential to continuity at every level of being.

The advice given is to move with the times; to accept and appreciate the profound gifts of life and death, of continuity and change, of increase and decrease; and to use them to the fullest while we can.

Changing Lines

Change in the first line: It flourishes like kudzu.

An interconnected system of loyalties and obligations may be choking off progress. If you wish to eradicate a stubborn and invasive element, it will be necessary to remove the entire network, roots and all. Take vigorous action. Join forces with people who truly are of your own kind. Through repeated and diligent effort, you can clear the way forward.

Change in the second line: This side of the river is nothing but swampland. Get across to the other side.

You are surrounded by ineffectual people who can only hinder you. It is time to move toward a more vibrant center of activity, a place where you truly belong, where your gifts can be recognized and valued and your goals achieved. Go now. When you make the decisive move, the people and ideas that have been holding you back will simply drop out of sight.

Change in the third line: The road goes uphill and down. You can't coast the whole way.

A time of difficulty lies ahead, but that shouldn't surprise you just because you've had it easy for a while. It's time to roll up your sleeves and step up to the work that must be done, no matter how tedious. You will be rewarded in due time, because you remain connected to your sense of purpose. So don't worry. Invest the sweat equity in this enterprise and enjoy the support of those who spur you on with their own best efforts.

Change in the fourth line: Like a fledgling fluttering its wings, afraid to leave the nest.

You allow timidity to hold you back, not for any good reason but only because you compare yourself to others who are better off than you in one way or another. So what? Enjoy your connections! Make the most of them! If you need help, ask! There are people who know your true worth and are willing to support your plans. They have faith in you; return the courtesy.

Change in the fifth line: A grand wedding.

This is a great union, a fusion of ideas that extends its influence down through the generations. Take joy and pleasure in the ceremony of it all. It signifies the fulfillment of your heart's desire.

Change in the top line: Don't use force to defend a dying ideal.

You may feel nostalgic about the time that's passing, but it is vital that you recognize the inevitable collapse of all things. If you can adjust to the new conditions you will be in a position to build something new. Remember the past, understand it, and relinquish it.

12

Stagnation

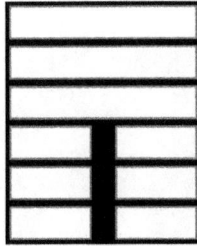

*When the rich get richer and the poor
get poorer, the prisons get bigger and
the streets get meaner.*

Associated concepts, images and attributes: Stagnation, regression, disconnection, misfortune, a lack of initiative, apathy, dysfunction, disquiet, dissatisfaction.

The Trigrams: Earth and Sky, each occupying its own position and going its own way, suggest a time of spiritual alienation, cultural stratification and inertia.

The atmosphere is one of devaluation and dissatisfaction, with a lack of cooperation between the elements of society. Within the individual, this might take the form of self-sabotage, malaise or a misalignment of desires. No matter how badly you may want something, nothing seems to come of your efforts to obtain or achieve it. Even if you do accomplish an aim, no good seems to come of it.

There is a warning implied here that you are heading down a wrong path; what lies this way will leave you isolated, not independent, downtrodden rather than supported. The ability to realize your goals will pass you by, and in its wake will come a time of meanness, lack and disappointment. The way to deal with the situation is to withdraw and bide your time. Don't give up on your plans, but take your hat out of the ring for now. This is neither your time nor your arena.

Changing Lines

Change in the first line: When roots are entangled, getting uprooted does not mean isolation.

Save those who can be saved. You need the company of those with whom you truly belong, and they need yours. Seek out your support system. Retreat from public life but maintain your most trusted connections. This makes it easier to bide your time and to keep the faith.

Change in the second line: Don't muddy the waters. Don't disturb the flock.

Accept your isolation with dignity. Be calm inwardly and don't bother other people with your opinions; they won't listen. Go your own way and let them go theirs. They may seem like a flock of sheep, wandering aimlessly in the swampy lowlands, but does that make you their shepherd?

Change in the third line: No way to act. Withdraw from yourself.

Do nothing. If you listen to your own conscience, you begin to understand that your impulses are less than honorable. Get a grip. Use the utmost restraint.

Change in the fourth line: A light in the darkness. An island in the swamp.

Times are bad, no doubt about that. Yet you have found something of real value that has the power to restore your faith. Make the most of this connection. Let it guide your behavior. In the end, this will bring you joy and satisfaction.

Change in the fifth line: Cross your fingers and your toes, too.

In the midst of a difficult time, a renewed sense of hope arrives and with it the worry that things won't pan out. See to the details. You have nothing to lose and everything to gain. Things may feel uncertain, but they are definitely turning around.

Change in the top line: The obstruction is undermined. The swamp is draining.

This was bound to happen sooner or later. A reversal of fortune appears suddenly and for the better—much better. Let go of the recent past; it's over and done. Step into the light and work to reclaim what you thought was lost.

13

The Social Network

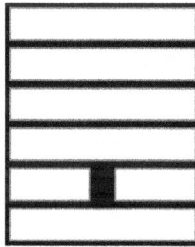

*It is a good and human thing to stand
under an open sky when the air is clear,
when there is warmth and light enough
for seeing and being seen.*

Associated concepts, images and attributes: Sociability, cooperation, collaboration, fellowship, networking, joint ventures, shared vision, common goals.

The Trigrams: Fire and Sky give rise to the image of a bonfire or an outdoor barbeque, a time of easy sociability, of building and maintaining relationships out in the open.

You are encouraged to connect and interact with all kinds of people. Find areas of agreement and ways to work together for mutual benefit. Don't just hang with the usual crowd; get out and mingle. Seek out new relationships, partnerships and associations. Join groups both online and off. If you can't find one that meets your needs, start one up that does and invite others to join you. Engage!

Changing Lines

Change in the first line: Get out of the house!

Take the first step. Initiate contact. This is definitely not a mistake.

Change in the second line: If you always stick with your own kind, the world shrinks around you.

There is something clannish or ingrown about this relationship or this way of thinking. You need to move outside the confines of your own circles, away from your habitual way of doing and seeing things. Seek out new influences, new sources of information and insight. If you don't, you'll end up thinking and feeling small.

Change in the third line: Smiling, nodding, shaking hands, holding a club behind your back.

You are not really interested in what the other person has to say, you just wait for an opportunity to strike back. You want the last word, but it could be your epitaph. Drop the defensive attitude or suffer the isolation that comes with it. You won't earn anyone's trust if you behave suspiciously yourself.

Change in the fourth line: The upper hand and the moral high ground.

You clearly have the upper hand in this relationship. So much so that you have no need whatsoever to act aggressively. When right and might coincide like this, your good fortune is a given.

Change in the fifth line: Tears of anguish, tears of joy.

You may have to work through a serious misunderstanding before you can achieve mutual trust, but such hard-won affection is a valuable thing when it results in true loyalty to a common cause.

Change in the top line: Five thousand of your closest friends.

You broaden your social circle and your sphere of influence. This is different from the warm relationships you cultivate within your inner circle, but there is real value in extending yourself to the wider group. There is nothing in this to regret.

14

Abundant Assets

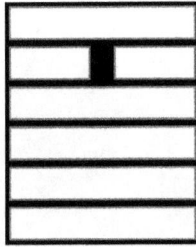

*The value of the sun rests not in what it
has but in what it sheds.*

Associated concepts, images and attributes: Great wealth,
influential connections, magnanimity, sharing of wealth,
benefaction.

The Trigrams: Sky and Fire suggest the radiance of the sun and
the blessings of heaven, a time of supreme good luck and
benevolence.

The arrangement of the hexagram is such that a single modest line
occupies a ruling position in the midst of others more powerful
than itself. The wealth you enjoy may lie outside your person, but
after all, that is the nature of possession. There are many ways in
which to be rich. The teaching of this auspicious hexagram is to
recognize and accept the value of your connections, which are
your most genuine assets.

There is a second meaning here as well. The sun appears small in relation to the vastness of the heavens. In fact, it is a modest star. But as the center of its own system, it holds the planets in orbit as it radiates its own warmth and energy outward, thereby making visible the beauty and mystery of each of those far-flung bodies. By shedding its own light, it simultaneously nourishes and calls attention to everything in its vicinity.

The advice therefore is twofold: Surround yourself with capable people and beneficial influences. Listen to wise counsel. At the same time, use your own radiance and influence to bring the achievements of others to light. You gain credit not by taking it but by giving it.

Changing Lines

Change in the first line: There is no harm to be found.

If you have any doubts about an association with someone or something, you can relax and enjoy the connection. There may be some hard work involved, but that's not a mistake, either. It leads to a successful outcome.

Change in the second line: Heavy-duty equipment.

You require a powerful vehicle—a big idea or a delivery system capable of carrying your plans and dreams to the next level. Because this is a time of abundance, the implication is that you have access to just such equipment or influence. Make use of powerful resources to do your bidding. Act with confidence. You won't fail.

Change in the third line: "Ask not what your country can do for you. Ask what you can do for your country." ~ John Fitzgerald Kennedy

Dedicate yourself to your noblest ideals, even if it involves a sacrifice. Nothing less will do. Petty motives and small-mindedness are of absolutely no use to you now.

Change in the fourth line: No declaration of war. No claim-staking.

You may be tempted to draw a line in the sand, but there is nothing to be gained by acting that way. You don't need to have your own way in this matter. Instead, bring out the qualities of others and of what they bring to the table. You won't be making a mistake if you can turn your hostile stance into a more inviting one.

Change in the fifth line: Your connection is a spiritual one. You make a good impression.

A trusting heart connects you at a deep level with those around you and above you. Everyone benefits from your actions now, so don't hold back. Act with the courage of your convictions, and nothing can stand in your way.

Change in the top line: Heaven smiles down on you.

You enjoy divine protection. Your plans, your people and your purpose find favor in high places. The way is open to you. Whatever you do now meets with success. Consider it a mandate from Heaven and you won't go wrong.

15

Stubborn Humility

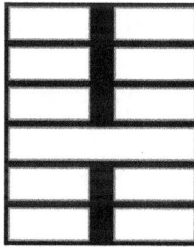

The mountain does not play King of the Mountain.

Associated concepts, images and attributes: Modesty, reverence, radical compliance, simplicity, earnestness, personal power.

The Trigrams: Mountain and Earth, because the one lies hidden within, or underneath, the other, suggest a deliberate lack of visible prominence, like that of a mountain so old and so eroded that it is no longer distinguishable from the surrounding plain.

Your value and effectiveness have nothing to do with appearances, status or possession. If you follow a conventional path, it is only because that is the most effective path to your goal. So powerful and central is the principle of stubborn humility to the achievement of any worthwhile goal that all of the lines of change in the current hexagram are favorable. If you can accept and use the energy of simplicity and earnestness in your approach to life, you can master any situation. Nothing can derail you, because you are the rail, not the locomotive; the direction, not the thing being directed. Does this require self-abnegation? It depends on how you think of yourself and what you identify with.

Changing Lines

Change in the first line: A humble birth.

Lacking privilege, you are required to make a more diligent effort. This is an entirely favorable situation. Your hard work makes you less likely to skip any steps, so the outcome will be better than anything that might have come more easily for you, and you are in a better position to understand the true benefits of what you have to offer. Make sure to double-check everything, then take the crucial step forward that you are contemplating. Unconscious powers are at work. Stay in the middle of the current.

Change in the second line: Voice recognition.

The work you are doing in private does not go unnoticed. You are like an animal calling out to others of its own kind, who recognize and answer it. Keep doing what you're doing. You don't have to think hard about it to know that it is both important and right.

Change in the third line: Doing work that matters, you don't have to advertise.

You are doing important work that is vitally connected to the needs of others. When you proceed in this way, your own needs are also met. So carry on.

Change in the fourth line: Cut through the red tape.

You don't let your own pride get in the way, so don't put up with pettiness from others if it threatens to hinder your work. If you can do this without getting attached to your own sense of righteous indignation, you will avoid damaging arguments. Then everything will fall into your hands.

Change in the fifth line: If you can't finance the undertaking yourself, use other people's money.

When it's time to expand, accept the help that is offered. Your purpose is real, and you have the support you need. Don't be deterred by insecurity or false modesty. Instead, attack the obstacles that confront you with everything at your disposal. It is not you alone who will benefit from your decisive action.

Change in the top line: Going viral.

People respond enthusiastically to the purpose you embody. You gain recognition for your work, not because it's about you, but because other people feel connected to it in the same that way you do. Gather that enthusiasm and use it to make a bold new push. The way will open to you.

16

Enthusiasm

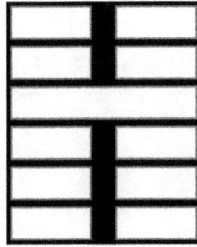

If you want people to think with you, give them a reason; if you want them to agree with you, give them a rhyme; but if you want them to get up and get moving, you've got to give them a rhythm.

Associated concepts, images and attributes: Emotional response, pleasure, mass appeal, crowds, music, dance, celebration, rousing speeches, salesmanship, showmanship, hypnotic suggestion; also, making provisions and preparations for celebration, exhibition or presentation.

The Trigrams: Earth and Thunder suggest a reverberation that is felt in the feet, a rousing, irresistible beat that inspires movement.

The structure of the hexagram for Enthusiasm is the inverse of that for Stubborn Humility, and for good reason. The emphasis here is on outward display rather than intrinsic worth. That is not to say, however, that the energy of enthusiasm cannot or ought not to be put to good use. A sham enthusiasm with nothing behind it will, of course, be exposed sooner or later, and a constant deluge of enthusiasm dulls the senses. But the spontaneous expression of joyous assent, even when the groundwork for it has been carefully laid, can inspire the masses and urge us on as individuals to greater achievement.

You are encouraged to consider the craft of promotion, the orchestration of an event of some kind, to pull back the curtain for a good look at the pulleys and levers of stagecraft. It may be that you need to learn how to make use of them or to understand your own susceptibility to advertising and other forms of persuasion. On the other hand, when something worth celebrating and promoting comes along, you are encouraged to pull out all the stops, strike up the band and dance to the music!

Changing Lines

Change in the first line: Trumped up enthusiasm. Name-dropping gets you nowhere fast.

Stop trying to convince people (including yourself) of your own importance by boasting about how well-connected you are. You won't get out of difficult straights by calling in favors or by calling out for help. That only exhausts the strength you have left. Put in the effort to build something of your own to brag about instead.

Change in the second line: Like a rock. Unencumbered by hustlers.

You can see to the heart of the situation and remain unmoved by the enthusiasm of the crowd. No need to weigh the pros and cons, just go about your business. If you can sustain this clarity of insight, you will have neither the need nor the inclination to flatter those in power, nor will you behave condescendingly toward those who are held in thrall by them.

Change in the third line: Held in thrall. Who hesitates is lost.

Try not to be so impressed by others that it robs you of the ability to act. Don't be skeptical of the way you feel, though. Your connection to this person, project or idea is not a mistake, unless you let it slip through your fingers. Pick up your jaw and show your support by getting to work.

Change in the fourth line: No doubt about it. Your enthusiasm is infectious.

You are in sync with a real source of power and enthusiasm. Your sincerity is attractive and energizing to others, who lend their support. Ride this wave! You can do great things with energy like this behind you.

Change in the fifth line: Even stifled enthusiasm serves a purpose; it keeps you alive.

Your vitality is compromised, so you are prevented from giving your all. This is like having a chronic illness that hinders you but, at the same time, keeps you from expending your energy in ways that might actually kill you. Not an ideal situation by any means, but not the end of the world.

Change in the top line: Dancing in the dark. Change your clothes, your hair, your face.

You may have given your enthusiasm prematurely or without good reason and are left feeling exhausted and, at the same time, wanting more. Let your dissatisfaction guide you toward something more fulfilling. Step out of the darkness and into the light. By changing the way you see yourself, you can shift the world around you to correspond with your new vision.

17

Following

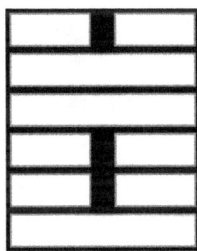

*If you want to be a good leader, learn
what it means to follow. If you want to
have a good following, teach what it
means to lead.*

Associated concepts, images and attributes: Influence, attraction,
guidance, natural inclination, assent, faithfulness, the path of life.
Adherence to a career, a tradition, a faith.

The Trigrams: Thunder and Lake, when their associated
meanings are paired in this arrangement, suggest a natural
stimulus and response like the harmonic resonance between the
strings of musical instruments that are tuned alike, or between
hearts that are similarly entrained.

The twin concepts of following and leading are like the two sides
of a spinning coin. If you want to gain a following, you must first
know how to follow. You must give support even as you enlist it,

encouraging others by first understanding their needs as well as you understand your own. Wherever you happen to be on a given path, there will be others ahead of you as well as behind. You serve those who come after you by keeping the path clear, and you keep the path clear by following it.

You are not required to go where everyone else is going, but if you decide to strike out on a path of your own, make sure that it leads somewhere promising and that you mark the way clearly; otherwise, you'll end up lost and alone. People naturally follow the path of least resistance, but if you provide a compelling reason to take a new course, those who understand will make the effort required of them. In such a case, however, simple persuasion is not enough; you must also lend clear guidance and assistance along the way.

Changing Lines

Change in the first line: Break camp. Go out and mingle.

You may hold a position of authority within your own camp, but now is the time to set out on your own. The way to do this is to get outside the confines of your own circle. Listen to the opinions and points of view of all kinds of people, those with whom you are inclined to disagree as well as those who already share your views. Accept challenges to your preconceptions. In this way you can find out what's truly needed in the world. What you learn from such thoughtful investigation has the power to inform your path in life.

Change in the second line: Following impulse and inexperience, you lose touch with wisdom.

You may feel a natural attraction to something fresh and new, but the enticement creates a fork in the road. Make your choice carefully now. If you follow this whim, it will separate you from a deeper, more meaningful influence.

Change in the third line: Following an experienced guide, you lose touch with youthful innocence.

Every choice means letting go of one thing or another. Don't worry; you have chosen wisely. Even though you may feel a certain loss, the time has come to let go of your attachment to someone or something that can no longer serve you. The more mature influence will lead you to the realization of your dreams.

Change in the fourth line: Following does not mean stalking. The way you are going leads you into a trap, but you can easily turn yourself around and get back on the path again.

You have turned following into a game of pursuit. You want something a bit too badly, and it is bound to lead you into real trouble, unless you wake up and get back to your true purpose. Once you do that, your head will clear. Remember why you set out on this path to begin with.

Change in the fifth line: Your compass is true.

You follow something that leads you on the path to real achievement. No need to second guess it. Your heartfelt attraction is like the needle of a compass. Your own magnetism points you to the source.

Change in the top line: *"Bodhisattva, I'm gonna sell my house in town." ~ Steely Dan*

You are deeply devoted to someone or something truly inspiring. This connection leads you further along your chosen path and inspires others to follow in your footsteps. Your future is so bright, and you are so firmly bound to it, that you can easily let go of anything that needlessly ties you down or binds you to the past, including material possessions and social connections.

18

The Bag of Shadows

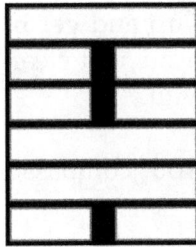

*As it is with the cosmologist who
studies the far-flung structures of the
universe, so it is with each of us when
we turn our scopes inward: so much of
what we thought was nothing at all
turns out to be riddled with dark matter
and sizzling with dark energy.*

Associated concepts, images and attributes: Corruption,
perversion, decadence, negativity, haunts, hallucinations,
disturbing dreams, the death of a parent and/or the effects of
parental abuse or negligence, guilt, shame, post-traumatic stress.
Redemption, forgiveness, reform.

The Trigrams: Wood and Mountain, with their connotations of
fertility on the one hand and inhibition on the other, suggest a

condition of perversion, rot and decadence that must be addressed. The means by which to affect reform are suggested as well, by the alternative associations with fresh air or penetrating wind and a firm resolve.

Untoward influences that may have been suppressed or hidden from view now step to the fore to be dealt with. Whether the blame rests with you or not, the affects of past mistakes (which may have their origins in previous generations) have manifested either within you or in such a way that the responsibility for correcting them now belongs to no one else. This does not mean that you must confront these demons alone; help is available to you. You are encouraged to make the most of it.

As a substance putrefies, its toxicity is gradually neutralized. This process can be helped along. To the extent that we are willing to expose old wounds to the healing effects of light and air — that is to say, of honest and open examination — we rid ourselves of their long-term ill effects. What doesn't kill us has the opportunity to make us stronger, but not the obligation. Determination and gentleness are required in the right combination and with the right timing, applied with thoughtful ruthlessness. Tough love for oneself is not to be confused with the internalization and perpetuation of abuse; nor does compassion serve us if it is allowed to devolve into laxity.

Changing Lines

Change in the first line: The sins of the father. It's up to you to redeem your good name.

Past abuses of power and authority have led to corruption in the present way of thinking. Trace persistent patterns of belief that do not serve you back to their source, without attaching blame to others or taking it on yourself. If you can manage this, new possibilities will emerge that are better aligned with your purpose. Be patient and unremitting in this.

Change in the second line: The sins of the mother. There is no quick fix.

This is not a time for bold initiatives. Treat this situation as you would a malnourished child, with a long-term commitment to patience, gentleness and provision. Trust has been disturbed at the most fundamental levels and must be re-established before anything else can be accomplished.

Change in the third line: Collusion and collaboration in the past. Anger and remorse in the present.

Remorse over your own participation in, or failure to stand up to, abuses of authority may lead to overzealous punishment of the perpetrators, including yourself. This is better than allowing things to continue as before, but it cuts you off from that which is truly needed — namely, reorientation and patient rehabilitation.

Change in the fourth line: Collusion and collaboration. You will have to face the music.

If you are not part of the solution, you are part of the problem. Change is coming; if you continue to tolerate and defend current abuses of authority or fail to lend your support to the corrective influences that are coming, you will find yourself cut off, lonely and desperate.

Change in the fifth line: Reformation and reclamation. Power and direction return.

You have the chance to institute changes that set things right again after a period of neglect and abuse. Your part in the process of revitalization will be recognized, and you will find a new sense of direction and purpose to move you forward.

Change in the top line: No time for political maneuvering. You operate on a different plane.

Temporal power, by its very nature, exerts a corrupting influence. The advice in the current situation is to steer clear of it. Your purpose is to find and serve something that endures beyond the current climate of opinion-mongering and jockeying for position. You will find greater rewards in following your own path.

19

Attraction

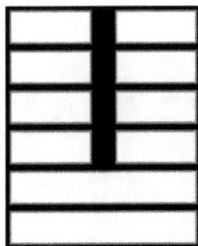

Life and the lust for it stir first in the
belly.

Associated concepts, images and attributes: Arrival, threshold, initiation, transition, proximity, visitation, contact, first stirrings of joy or passion, mutual attraction, closeness of or to the spiritual realm, divination, augury. Also, a way, path or manner of approach.

The Trigrams: Lake and Earth, suggesting joy and burial, indicate a suppressed excitement that manages nevertheless to make itself felt.

Something profound and awe-inspiring moves toward you, desirous of contact. This may make itself felt as the first stirrings of a new interest or obsession, a fleeting or tantalizing flirtation or a deeper sense of longing, an omen or the appearance of an important person or symbol in your dreams.

You have been issued an invitation. You may respond by taking a step closer yourself, accepting and remaining open to the new influence without harboring a particular expectation or agenda of your own.

Changing Lines

Change in the first line: The attraction is mutual. Moving with it opens a door.

You possess a spiritual affinity with this new element. So much so that the situation is imbued with a sense of reunion, as if something from which you have been separated is only now returning. Don't rush things; remain open to the idea of gradual re-acquaintance.

Change in the second line: The attraction is mutual. It's all good.

You possess a strong bond with this new and inspiring element, and only good will come of it. You need have no fear of the future.

Change in the third line: A sweet thing approaches. Beware of it!

A tantalizing opportunity makes itself available to you, but no good will come of it. Easy acceptance leads to bitter regret. The choice to let it pass, while difficult and maybe even painful, will spare you a greater sense of remorse down the road. The sooner you get over this idea, the better, because there is no lasting connection to be had.

Change in the fourth line: Climax approaches. Don't hold back.

Commit yourself to this impulse or influence. It is not a mistake and it will not harm you. This is certainly no time for self-conscious behavior or half-hearted measures. Give it all you've got.

Change in the fifth line: Attracted to wisdom. The qualities of true leadership emerge.

Your approach to those capable of genuine support frees them to act with initiative and independence that furthers the common good. Act with confidence in them and in your plans. Do this now. By demonstrating such maturity, you in fact acquire it.

Change in the top line: Magnanimous attraction. Great blessings flow from it.

A deep and abiding joy in life proceeds from just such generosity as this. Being free of need yourself, you are able to give freely to others, with the result that both you and they are enriched, and nothing at all of what you truly value is depleted. In fact, your own aims are furthered along with everyone else's.

20

Point of View

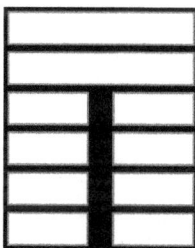

Before you command anyone or
anything else, you must gain a
commanding view: of yourself first, and
second, of your environment.

Associated concepts, images and attributes: Observation, contemplation, view, seeing and being seen, self-reflection, oversight. An observatory, watchtower, or antenna. Radio waves, broadcast communication.

The Trigrams: Earth and Wood, in their current arrangement, give rise to the image of a tower or platform rising above the earth. A second image is suggested by the arrangement of the lines, which emanate downwards like the beacon of a satellite, both receiving and transmitting information across vast distances.

Now is the time not for action but for contemplation based on a free flow of information. Allow yourself the space and time you need in order to take everything into account. This is not a luxury but a necessity. Ponder things deeply. When you achieve the perspective needed to truly understand the situation, you will be in a better position to deliver your message effectively and to make yourself understood.

Changing Lines

Change in the first line: A child's eye view.

Your current perspective is limited. If someone else is calling the shots, there is no harm in this, but if you are in a position to make important decisions, you need to develop a deeper, more mature understanding of the situation. Your actions have implications and repercussions that can leave you looking quite the fool, otherwise.

Change in the second line: The view through a keyhole.

Your view is obstructed. When you look at things from a suspicious point-of-view, trying to obtain information in a furtive or underhanded way, you needlessly limit your field of vision. This is not only shameful but ultimately self-injurious. If there is information you truly need, find a way to ask for it that is neither manipulative nor deceptive.

Change in the third line: Re-envisioning your life. You have a choice.

Take the opportunity to look back over the course of your life, at the decisions that have led you to your current view of yourself and of your life. You enter into a transitional phase in which it is possible to reinvent yourself. When you begin to see your situation as one of many possible outcomes of the exercise of free will, you are empowered to create exactly the future you want.

Change in the fourth line: Through the eyes of a guest. A detached point of view has its advantages.

Try looking at your situation through the eyes of a well-meaning visitor. It is possible to inhabit the moment fully without being emotionally trapped in it. Does your entire life hinge on what you do or say now? Remember that you are only a guest in this world. Be respectful, but lighten up a little and enjoy the sights.

Change in the fifth line: Seeing into the mirror without blame.

Seeing yourself in human terms grounds you in the world. Accept the commonality of experience as your strength. Consider your actions and their consequences and learn from them; then you may commit yourself to a course of action that will be of benefit.

Change in the top line: Seeing out from the mirror without blame.

The shift in point of view from the previous line to the current one is subtle but profound. In both cases, the effect is one of compassionate accountability, but when one is able to see the pattern of one's life from a standpoint wholly devoid of egocentricity — from the point of view of the other, of the greater self who abides as one's constant companion and observer — then questions of right and wrong resolve themselves of their own accord, and duality is eliminated.

21

The Bridle

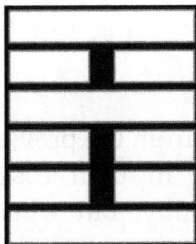

*Punishment ought to follow the
revelation of a crime the way thunder
follows lightning – ideally with a little
counting space between the two events.
A rush to judgment is indicative of
immediate danger, not only to the one
whose house is struck but to the whole
neighborhood.*

Associated concepts, images and attributes: Crime and punishment, chewing on a problem, biting through or grinding down an obstacle, tenacity, determination, law enforcement, investigation, litigation, prosecution, rehabilitation.

The Trigrams: Quake and Fire suggest thunder and lightning. The arrangement of solid and broken lines gives rise to a second image: that of an open mouth with a barrier between the teeth that interferes with intelligible speech or with telling the truth, but which, like a bit attached to a bridle, may well be useful in terms of controlling and directing behavior.

Ideas of crime and punishment are invoked, as well as the resolution of difficult or stubborn problems, often in communication between two or more people or in terms of being honest with oneself. The problem may be one of addiction or denial of a significant, relevant fact or situation. Persistent and determined effort is required to get at the problem, to break it down or analyze it, and to dissolve it.

In terms of specific advice, the hexagram suggests that legal action may be required or that a painstaking attitude might be employed with success, with the added injunction that any punishment to be meted out ought to be commensurate with the crime. A warning against illegal or immoral behavior, including excessive punishments or uses of force, is implied.

Changing Lines

Change in the first line: Handcuffs and leg-irons. If you are lucky, there will be no prosecution.

Your mobility may be limited by external control or limitations, but this is a good thing. You may have been caught in the act (or you may have caught yourself in time), before you were able to carry out a harmful or unwise intention. This is fortunate. You can learn a valuable lesson. Be grateful. Use the period of inactivity to formulate a better plan.

Change in the second line: Biting down so hard that the nose disappears.

You tackle the problem at hand with great enthusiasm. So much so that you go a little overboard. The finer sensibilities (represented by the sense of smell) are blotted out, but this is not such a terrible mistake. You do the right thing in acting with such conviction.

Change in the third line: Biting down on salted meat. The whistleblower tastes poison.

You encounter an old and potentially dangerous problem that has been hidden from view. This releases a bitterness that needs to be aired. If you simply swallow it, it will do you real harm. By bringing things to light, you may arouse a poisonous hatred against yourself, but you will have to deal with the consequences either way. Better to bring the danger out in the open. If you allowed its effects to work on you internally, you would not easily recover from the damage.

Change in the fourth line: Grinding on metal. An arduous investigation.

In the course of your work, you discover something important and durable. Due diligence yields a reward beyond anything you might have expected. Do your research. Dig out the salient facts and don't rest until you understand their relevance and their implications.

Change in the fifth line: Grinding on gold. Adversaries come out of the woodwork, make no mistake.

As a result of your hard work, something of great value comes to light. This naturally arouses opposition and competition. If you can remain impartial and avoid over-reacting, you can step up to the challenges and prevail against false claims. If, in the process, you arouse your own inner demons as well, you will need to hear them out just as you would an adversary in a court of law. Separate fact from fiction in the stories you tell yourself, as well as in the narratives of others.

Change in the top line: Locked up for good. Your appeal will not be heard.

This involves a habitual pattern of behavior that will land you in serious trouble and cut you off from your sources of support. Like one who is locked up in an isolation chamber, with no way of understanding the larger situation, you may have difficulty accepting this news. Nevertheless, denial and excuses will only perpetuate the problem.

22

Design

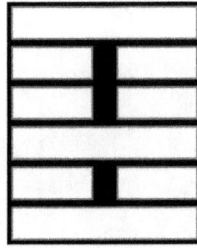

Grace is achieved when a quiet,
elevated manner is illuminated by a
fire down below.

Associated concepts, images and attributes: Elegance, grace, beauty, embellishment, polish, finish, form as an expression of content.

The Trigrams: Fire and Mountain suggest the illumination from within of that which is essential, prominent and durable.

While the emphasis here is on the outward appearance or presentation of an idea, the very concept of design implies an aesthetic that is married to intrinsic value or function. Tastes are both idiosyncratic and subject to fashion, but the important thing is to bring out the essential qualities of an item, a person or a project in such a way as to signify or to make visible that which is not readily apparent. This might be accomplished through elaboration, symbol, metaphor, story or illustration or by means of frank simplicity. However you go about it, you are encouraged to consider the way you frame an idea, the details of its execution and the manner of its exhibition, since presentation is an important element in its overall success.

Changing Lines

Change in the first line: Step out of the limousine and go on foot.

You will make better progress if you make your own way under your own power than if you accept the help of power and influence. Do not sacrifice your independence for the sake of comfort and ease.

Change in the second line: Growing out one's hair. Developing patience.

The hair may symbolize growth and power, individuality or superficiality. It emerges from within, yet it can be changed to reflect a new influence, style or stage of development. Patience is advised, since the change you anticipate will come about gradually. Allow things to develop naturally. In time, you will be able to make the best possible presentation.

Change in the third line: Saturated and impregnated. The pattern of perpetual life.

This follows the principle of fertility and the design of life. Cling to it like the fetus clings to the womb, and it will nourish you and your offspring in perpetuity.

Change in the fourth line: She'll be coming 'round the mountain. She'll be riding six white horses.

A team of six horses symbolizes the power and grace of the hexagram as a whole, with the ability to ascend to great heights; the color white suggests both purity and simplicity. A powerful and perhaps frightening connection is offered. Do not be put off by its sudden, strange appearance. Rather than rob you of power, this new influences seeks to ally itself with you.

Change in the fifth line: Receiving an engraved invitation, you bring a small gift and a contrite expression, all of which portends good fortune.

You are welcomed into a rather exclusive group of influential people. Being the newcomer, it may seem as if you have little to offer, and this is embarrassing at first. Don't let that stop you. You are in a fortunate position, and in time, things will turn around.

Change in the top line: Simplicity, simplicity, simplicity.

The very highest stage of design development is approached. Brilliance means the perfect union of form and function. The stark nature of unembellished truth is revealed in all its beauty.

23

Recycling

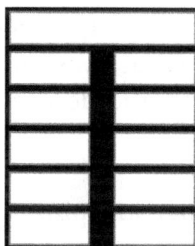

When the life goes out of a thing, we carve a monument and set it in the earth. Rigidity marches first in the parade, followed by rot; and rot, in turn, by new fertility.

Associated concepts, images and attributes: Separation, divorce, death, stripping away the old, skinning, flaying, cutting away, removing waste, clearing.

The Trigrams: Earth and Mountain provide the image of a headstone or a skeleton, with the associated image of a deathbed.

Outmoded forms, relationships, habits and ideas that no longer serve us need to be stripped down, dismantled and repurposed or — where that's not possible — discarded. The clutter and detritus of life, if not removed, only hampers new growth and movement. This is an essential part of the natural cycle of life. A rigid adherence to tradition, habit or possessions results in decay and an inability to adapt to new circumstances. The suggestion here is that something is worn out and has begun to disintegrate. The thing to do is not to start a new project but to set to work getting rid of what no longer works. This will release bound up, stagnant energy and restore vitality to a stalled project or relationship or, failing that, make room for a new one.

Changing Lines

Change in the first line: Stripping the deathbed.

Something related to the most basic issues of intimacy and trust has passed. It is time, no matter how painful the occasion, to strip away the reminders of what was and to give the matter a thorough airing. Otherwise, the decay of the old will infect and inhibit the new.

Change in the second line: Stripping the bed and changing the frame.

It is not enough to change your surroundings or relationships when the underlying structure of your life is in disrepair. The most basic framework upon which you build relationships of the kind in question is fundamentally flawed. Change the way you see things from the ground up. Imagine not just the next new thing, but an entirely new kind of thing. Institute the changes in your own view of things that will make possible what you truly need and want in your life. Old habits of thought and behavior must be replaced with new ones.

Change in the third line: Strip it away. There is nothing to blame.

Never mind who or what was at fault. Dwelling on the past will only hinder you. The important thing is to get rid of the old and to do it now. What does it matter if someone else holds you responsible? Be responsible! Out with the old, in with the new!

Change in the fourth line: Like stripping away your own skin. Like recycling your own flesh and blood.

In the course of a major renovation, it is important not to get carried away. You are cutting too close to the bone, getting rid of something that is vital to your own well-being. This is a mistake that will cost you dearly if you go through with it.

Change in the fifth line: Gentleness in recycling. Fertility returns.

Here the idea of stripping away shifts subtly in the direction of inviting the new. This is not an aggressive seduction but a flirtation or courting of a new idea or relationship. Allowing it will open you to a fertile cycle of thought and activity that holds promise for the future, provided you continue to let yourself be led and do not try to assume control.

Change in the top line: A ripe fruit, ready to peel. A moving van is available. If you stay where you are, your house will fall apart.

You hold the future in the palm of your hand. Peel it and eat it. Big changes await you. You can take everything that is truly valuable with you and establish a new life on your own terms. If you merely try to renovate your current situation, you will fail. You can't prop up a rotten structure with a coat of paint.

24

Reversal

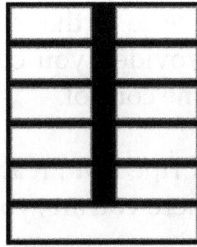

*The road you have taken is never the
wrong one, provided you have the power
to reverse direction.*

Associated concepts, images and attributes: Revival, resurgence, rebirth, new energy, Spring, reversal, return, recovery, restoration.

The Trigrams: Stimulus and Earth, with a single strong line emerging from the bottom and open, receptive lines all the way up, suggest ideas of return and rebirth. The earth, stimulated from beneath by the germination of plants, returns to life in the Spring.

A resurgence of energy is available for a new beginning. It is important to reconnect with the most vital elements of your plan while making room for new ideas to emerge. You may have lost your way or made a wrong turn, but all is not lost. Retrace your steps, correct any errors you may have made, reunite with former friends or associates, do what it takes to get back on track. It is important to have a clear goal in mind. This keeps you oriented even as you do the necessary backtracking.

Changing Lines

Change in the first line: The way back is easy.

You may feel isolated and distanced from your goal or sense of purpose, but in fact, you have not strayed far. You can easily get back to the path. Just reorient yourself and go! It really is as simple as that, but the longer you wait, the more difficult it will seem.

Change in the second line: Relax and return. Be human about it.

The cause of your worry is clear enough. You've tried something that isn't working out. Mistakes and course corrections are part of the process, so let go of the need to be right and get back to the place where you can try something new. Be humble enough to talk about what's happened, and you may find that you've actually learned something valuable.

Change in the third line: Urgent return from the brink. Master yourself.

You've come close to a real disaster. Fortunately, you can recognize the situation for what it is and you are able to step back from the edge in time. This may require a certain level of self-abnegation or the relinquishing of a cherished ideal, but you can see where the pursuit of an unrealistic or inappropriate dream would actually lead. You can avoid a serious mistake if you turn around in time.

Change in the fourth line: Return to yourself, even if you have to go it alone.

What is centermost in your life is shifting. This means that you must change your direction, with or without the approval and cooperation of others. March to the beat of your own heart.

Change in the fifth line: Returning home and sharing the wealth.

At the conclusion of a successful campaign, you have the wherewithal to give generously to your base of support. This allows for the perpetuation of renewal. Reinvest your profits, not selfishly, but in order to benefit the greatest number of people.

Change in the top line: Blind to the possibility of returning, you drive on. You will be lost for a very long time.

You hurtle blindly down the wrong road, incapable of admitting your mistake. How long before you realize that you don't recognize where you are, much less how to get back? If you undertake to lead a group endeavor in this way, you will make a blunder of grand proportions. There is no gps signal that can help you, because the flaw is in your own ability to navigate. The sooner you stop and humbly ask for guidance, the better off you'll be.

25

Spontaneity

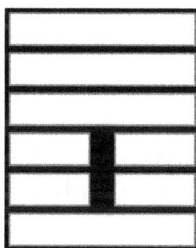

*Spontaneity is so often punishable in children
that we grow up flinching from it in adulthood.
There is no need to learn spontaneity;
train the mind, instead, to be
unflinching.*

Associated concepts, images and attributes: Disentanglement, childlike innocence, self-confidence, purity, directness, trust, release from inhibition.

The Trigrams: Shock and Sky suggest a stimulus that arises from within, combined with the freedom to respond creatively.

Spontaneous behavior that springs naturally from a heart free of entanglement and negativity has the full support of the emotional and spiritual realms and therefore the greatest possibility of success, while those impulses that arise from fear, lust, envy, hatred or any of the myriad permutations of distrust meet with resistance and sabotage from within and without.

As a casualty of the process of socialization, often as a result of emotional trauma, the individual often loses the capacity to act spontaneously, with childlike faith in oneself and in the world. Recovering that ability requires of us that we disentangle the network of negative emotions and patterns of behavior that cling to and inhibit or pervert the natural urges. Self-restoration means weeding out that which arises from reactive impulse in order to allow intuition to flourish, eradicating compulsion in order to liberate spontaneity, and shaking ourselves free of obsession so that we may recognize innate creativity.

Changing Lines

Change in the first line: Disentangle yourself and make your move.

When your intentions are free of negativity, you are free to do as you like. Your actions will align with a genuine sense of purpose.

Change in the second line: Effortless abundance. Attend to the process.

A seeming paradox is implied here. The way to achieve what you want is to care more about the process of its creation than the result of it. Staying in the flow of your work is its own reward. Let that be enough for now, and the external rewards will follow.

Change in the third line: Key in the ignition, a full tank of gas. Lucky for the one who needs to get somewhere, not so lucky for the one who parked the car.

The principle of ownership and questions of legality notwithstanding, the energy and ability to accomplish something have been made available, but they should not be regarded as your personal possessions. If you identify with the one looking to get somewhere, you can seize the opportunity and go. If you identify with the victim, whether you are to blame or not, you suffer the loss of mobility.

Change in the fourth line: Free of entanglements. Empowered.

You are not mistaken in your plans. Go through with them.

Change in the fifth line: An unexpected affliction. Don't try to remedy it.

The situation is like an illness from a virus that you happened to catch. It's not your fault, and there's really nothing you can do about it. Be patient. It will run its course and be done with you, then you'll feel better.

Change in the top line: Spontaneous action leads to disaster and exhaustion of resources.

Even though you are inherently free of negativity, external conditions are not conducive to your plans. The timing is wrong, it's as simple as that.

26

The Battery

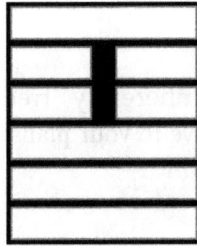

*The difference between creation and
annihilation depends not on the amount
or kind of force but on its containment.*

Associated concepts, images and attributes: Restraint, inhibition, domestication, sublimation.

The Trigrams: Sky and Mountain, by virtue of the volatility of the former and the immovability of the latter, give rise to images of power and containment: a dormant volcano, a genie in a bottle, a fully charged battery, a nuclear weapon.

The power at your disposal is considerable and worthy of your respect. It must be contained when not in use, its release managed with a firm hand. If such force were to be unleashed thoughtlessly, it could easily wreak havoc. Having a fixed goal toward which to strive enables the patient husbanding of resources. If you can take the long view and avoid wasting those resources prematurely, you can build influence and gather support.

The time is right for the accumulation of energy, strength and support in a controlled manner and for a specific, worthy purpose.

Changing Lines

Change in the first line: Accumulating enmity. You head into dangerous territory.

The course of action you are contemplating arouses negative emotions that have lain dormant for a long time. If you can bring things to a head and release the pent up energy in a safe manner, then do nothing further, you will be better off.

Change in the second line: Cork the bottle, decommission the vehicle, protect the cargo.

It is vital that you restrain your ambition by making it impossible to advance. You have something of great value that needs your protection and care. The time is not right to expose it to danger. If you demonstrate courage and devotion to your purpose in this way, you will accumulate the power you need to make a move when conditions are more favorable.

Change in the third line: Like a convoy of big rigs. Keep on trucking!

Things are in motion, one after another. You are in pursuit of an important goal. Think of yourself as hauling valuable cargo in an enclosed container. Close ranks with those you trust and keep your wits about you to ward off hijackers.

Change in the fourth line: A field of dreams: in the bullpen warming up, a young pitcher with a good arm will give you reason to celebrate.

The game isn't over. You have strength and skill at your disposal, like a baseball team with great depth in its pitching staff. You still have difficult work ahead of you, but in the end you'll be smiling and laughing.

Change in the fifth line: The bomb has been defused. Good fortune.

You have managed to disable a potentially destructive force that threatened to shut down your operation, turning a perilous situation into a personal triumph. You can move forward now.

Change in the top line: The force is with you. Success.

Forward motion is unimpeded. It is as if an unseen hand has removed every impediment to your success.

27

The Open Mouth

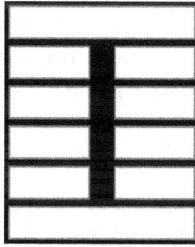

When you speak, think of your audience
as dinner guests. Serve others first, then
yourself. Leave the last morsel on the
plate and the final word unspoken.

Associated concepts, images and attributes: The jaws, teeth, and tongue; eating and speaking; provision of nourishment and wisdom; chewing; digestion; rumination.

The Trigrams: Shock and Mountain, the mobile and the stationary, give rise to an image of the lower and upper jaws, or an open mouth.

Your sources of nourishment, both bodily and spiritual, exert a profound influence on your physical, intellectual and spiritual metabolism. Your effectiveness in each area of your life depends on input as well as output. Often, the most refined food is the least nutritious. The same might be said of conventional wisdom, received knowledge and unexamined opinion. Seek balance in your diet and in your intelligence-gathering, and don't neglect to take in plenty of raw information in the form of direct study and observation. Check your facts and take as much time as you need in coming to your own conclusions. Don't just swallow everything that comes your way.

Be as careful of the words that leave your mouth as you are of the food you put in it. Speak from a thoughtful and sincere heart.

Changing Lines

Change in the first line: A drooping jaw. Salty tears mingle with your saliva. You've lost your Superman cape, tossed out your Wonder Woman cuffs.

You look at the fortunes of others with envy and self-pity, imagining yourself at a disadvantage. This is truly unfortunate, because it means that you have lost sight of your own power. You can do better. In fact, you must. Such suffering is insufferable.

Change in the second line: An open mouth, eyes turned upward.

Acting like a chick in the nest that waits to be fed, or like a sycophant hanging on the words of the master, is unworthy and undignified. Take responsibility, provide for yourself, do your own thinking!

Change in the third line: Biting the hand that feeds you, gnawing your own flesh.

You reject the source of true inspiration, wisdom and nourishment. This not only leaves you hungering after inappropriate and insubstantial distractions, it cuts you off from your own vital energy. This way lies addictive behavior that will do you real harm.

Change in the fourth line: The hungry tiger hunts best. Climbing the mountain, scouring the landscape for something to eat.

Your ferocious appetite is not a mistake. In fact, it elevates not only your game but your frame of reference. Keep at it. Keep searching for anything and everything that feeds your passion.

Change in the fifth line: Leaving the path in search of food, you will find what you seek. It's enough to feed you.

There are times when leaving others behind and venturing off on your own is the only way to find what you need. This might mean abandoning a way of life, the rules by which most people live, or the conventional path to success. This is not a mistake. You will make important discoveries and connections that will sustain you. The situation does not, however, lend itself to starting new projects that require the support of others.

Change in the top line: Drinking at the source. You will be rewarded for stepping into the current.

You are connected to ancient and primal sources of wisdom. Because of this, you have much to offer others; and you, in return, will be enriched. The difficulties you face will empower you. The generosity of the universe is yours to draw upon and to share.

28

The Roof Beam

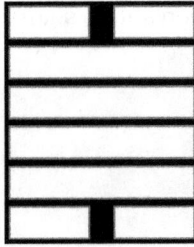

The constitution – of a nation or of an individual – is like a roof: good for protection against elemental nature, but only so long as it has support from underneath. Otherwise, it must be suspended.

Associated concepts, images and attributes: An inadequate social structure or way of life, a sagging roof or protective covering, lack of shelter, a faulty support system, imminent collapse, impending crisis.

The Trigrams: Wood and Lake suggest the image of a sagging roof that pools water instead of shedding it.

The structure of your life—or of some aspect of it that has previously provided cover, shelter or protection against external, elemental forces—is weakened and in danger of collapse. The crisis can be averted but only if you make a move quickly to get out of harm's way or to replace or fortify the supporting elements.

This may indicate any major life-changing event such as a change in employment or career; a change of marital, social or financial status; a new home or living conditions; the loss of a parent, sibling, spouse, mentor or other significant figure; a crisis of faith or identity; or a shift in values, philosophy, or way of life. Such changes, even when they are regarded as positive or necessary, create stresses that can result in a state of paralysis or collapse. This is not a time for endless debate or indecision. Immediate intervention is required.

Changing Lines

Change in the first line: Bubble wrap and sturdy boxes, preparing for the move.

Just as you might wrap the dishes and other fragile items to cushion them and prevent breakage during a move from one house to another, it is important to take great care in preparation for a new endeavor. The admonition is to act in small ways to protect and preserve what is most valuable. Consider what you want to bring with you from the past into the future. Pay careful attention to your most fundamental needs and motivations.

Change in the second line: A phoenix emerges from its ashes. A forest fire clears the way for new growth.

It often happens that, after suffering a great catastrophe, we are able to see not only that it was inevitable but also the real good that has come of it. The lesson in loss is to trust in the process of change. It will renew you, if you allow it.

Change in the third line: The roof beam buckles and snaps. You can't brace it up.

There is nothing you can do to avert disaster now. Attempting to stave off the crisis only puts you in greater danger. Move out of harm's way and make your peace with the change.

Change in the fourth line: The beam is braced at both ends. It's not a good time to add a second story.

You have come through the crisis in good shape. The structure of your life is stabilized and beautified. Enjoy your good fortune but don't try for more. That would only add stress and confusion, putting everything at risk again.

Change in the fifth line: Petals of rust amid the rubble. Nothing to celebrate, nothing to bemoan.

There is a certain beauty to be enjoyed even in decay. This is hardly a sign of renewal, but at least there's nothing left to lose.

Change in the top line: The roof collapses. Going in means going down in the flames.

All is truly lost. There is no judgment of any kind attached to this line. You are working to rescue what you can, even though your efforts will only result in greater loss. The image here is that of a firefighter entering a burning building from which he will not emerge again. Questions of heroism and self-sacrifice have no satisfactory answers. You are not required to go through with this, and you will not succeed. While there is no blame in going forward, there is certainly no shame in turning back.

29

The Gorge

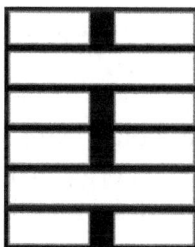

Experience is the best teacher, and the worst — the best because it teaches the same lessons again and again to every man, woman and child who takes the course; the worst because it does not care whether its lessons are heeded or not.

Associated concepts, images and attributes: High risk, repeated danger, rapid forward motion, a narrow passage, steep descent, white water, turbulence, taking the plunge, moving with the flow, responsiveness, staying in the moment.

The Trigrams: Water Repeated suggests the repetition of danger, giving rise to the image of a swift and turbulent river that presents one danger after another as it carves it way through a steep gorge.

The Gorge represents a highly volatile situation with little breathing space between one crisis and the next, a test of one's nerve, abilities, stamina, intelligence and will. The way to get through this time is to commit to it fully, holding nothing back, to take the plunge, to conquer fear. The only teacher in such a situation is the repetition of danger itself, within the specific flow of events.

The nature of water is not to climb out of danger but to accept it joyfully, to rest when there is a space in which to rest, to occupy the space that is empty until it is full, and to move on without hesitation. In this way, being true to itself, a stream acquires enough force to carve its own path, to undermine the most stubborn obstacles and to remain ceaselessly active until its journey is complete.

Practice, train hard, face your fears of inadequacy. You are connected to a vital spiritual energy that motivates you to do your best. Accept the challenge and the honor that goes with it.

Changing Lines

Change in the first line: A circular response. You are caught in an eddy.

Responding to the same kind of crisis in the same way over and over, you get caught up in a pattern of behavior that will only pull you down into hopelessness and despair. Try a daring new approach to an old problem. Give it everything you've got.

Change in the second line: Steep walls on either side. By staying in the middle, you make a little headway.

This is a strategic and unavoidable moment. Deadlines and the demands of others are closing in on you. Keep your central purpose firmly in mind. Do not allow yourself to be distracted by secondary concerns, but do remain adaptable to the flow of events and be satisfied with small gains.

Change in the third line: A steep drop to the left, another to the right. Either way you go, you will drown. Pull back hard!

This is more than you can handle. Any move you make will take you over the edge. You won't recover. The only thing to do is to stop your forward motion. Get out of the situation at all costs and wait until a genuine solution presents itself.

Change in the fourth line: Up the creek without a paddle. A flask of wine and a piece of bread, dropped down from above.

You are cut off, unable to rescue yourself. For the moment, at least, you are safe enough. Though it may not seem like enough, you have what you need. Help comes when you most need it and least expect it. In this, there is an element of divine providence.

Change in the fifth line: A quiet pool. The basin has filled up to the rim, but it's not spilling over yet.

While this is not a moment of crowning achievement, at least the danger is behind you, and you can go on with your life. In the calm of the moment, since you are no longer fighting merely to stay alive, your real purpose can come clear again.

Change in the top line: The river is entrenched. Hauled out of the gorge and thrown in prison. Bound and judged.

An entrenched river is one that has carved a bed so deep that it no longer has the ability to alter its course. By disregarding one's innate moral compass repeatedly, one deprives oneself of behavioral options. In such cases, outside forces (in the form of natural law or human authority) step in, and the individual's freedom is restricted even further. What you are contemplating represents a serious offense against yourself, someone else or possibly both. It will not be treated lightly. If you go on like this, you will be taken out of action permanently. Reconsider.

30

Lucidity

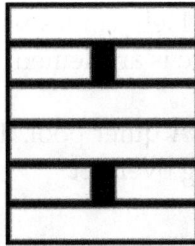

We need both in order to see, but we
place a greater premium on light than
on darkness because there is less of it in
the world. There is less of it because it
requires energy to produce.

Associated concepts, images and attributes: Mental clarity, brilliance, radiance, awareness, the light of day, fire, warmth combined with adherence to principle, shedding and spreading light.

The Trigrams: Fire Repeated gives rise to the image of the sun and signifies insight and illumination of the most durable kind.

As the unifying source of light and warmth upon which all life depends, the sun represents the divinity that is inherent in our being human. You are asked to display this quality now, to share it without reservation or partiality. Be articulate. Bring what is hidden to light, clarify that which is obscure, use gentleness to expose the truth that has been bound up in lies. Employ the faculty of reason—not calculating or manipulative logic but an attitude of compassionate illumination—to unify rather than separate.

The situation calls for a clear head and a warm heart.

Changing Lines

Change in the first line: Polishing the lens. Respect your vision.

Be open about your motives from the very beginning. There are cross-purposes at work in the early stages of an enterprise, but if you can articulate your vision so that others understand it clearly and know precisely what you want, you will avoid any costly mistakes. People can join with you in confidence only if you lead the way in setting aside any separatist agendas that might subvert or complicate your aims.

Change in the second line: Yellow light. Radiance is yours.

The way forward is brilliantly illuminated. You possess the clarity of heart and mind that will lead you to good fortune.

Change in the third line: In the light of the setting sun, awareness comes at last. You have a choice: to sing your song or to bemoan your fate.

The brevity of life is part and parcel of its beauty. In the face of death, we can use the light that remains to express the sweetness of the gift of life, or we can complain about it to the bitter end. It is entirely a matter of choice.

Change in the fourth line: A big flash of light. Blinking, blinking. It burns itself out in fifteen minutes.

A sudden flash of insight or mental clarity needs to be captured before it is lost. Sudden fame or wealth, in the absence of anything substantive to sustain it, is quickly spent. Carefully consider whether this is something that will fuel you for the long haul. If not, don't waste your time with it.

Change in the fifth line: Cry me a river. The tears will clarify your vision.

It might seem that your problems are magnified by your emotional state, but in fact your tears only bring to light a deep longing for a connection that you thought was lost. Let your sorrow change your perspective. If a river of tears is what it takes to reconnect you with something or someone of importance, in the end you will be smiling.

Change in the top line: Clear-headed execution. Decapitate the opposition. Capture the following.

In confronting and disabling your enemies, it is vital that you separate leaders from followers. Deal effectively and with finality in the case of the former, while reaching out to the latter. If you indulge the aims of those who seek to destroy you, you display a lack of confidence in your own mission, but if you can incorporate the legitimate views and concerns that fueled your opposition in the first place, you can add to your own base of support.

31

Influence

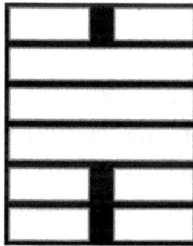

*If you want to influence the future,
make a lap.*

Associated concepts, images and attributes: Influence, excitation, mobilization, provocation, flirtation, stimulus and response, trigger, mutual or universal attraction.

The Trigrams: Mountain and Lake suggest an elevated or sublimated state of pleasure induced by stillness within and happiness in external matters.

The law of universal attraction applies in every area of life, to matters of great import and in things that may seem insignificant. You are encouraged in the present instance to make use of the pleasure principle as a means of attracting others or, conversely, to respond to an invitation from an element that actively seeks to influence you.

Not every source of influence or attraction is beneficial, of course. In general, that which is stable (symbolized by the mountain) tends to exert a greater influence upon the more fluid or volatile element (the lake, which sits in the crater or lap of the mountain). For this reason, movement or change in the lower lines is seen as less auspicious than movement in the upper lines, especially the fourth and fifth. There, responsiveness is more appropriate. In any case, keep an open mind; be approachable; respond from a centered heart.

Changing Lines

Change in the first line: Happy feet. You feel the beat in your big toe.

A new impulse or influence stirs your creative juices. Like a rhythm you can't ignore, it makes you want to get up and move. There is no way to know where it will lead you, but you definitely feel a connection. Right now, you're just tapping your foot.

Change in the second line: Feeling the impulse in your calves. It will trip you up.

A knee-jerk reaction will cause you to stumble. You want to make a move, but this is no way to start. So long as the influence is only a felt thing, it causes no harm, but as a basis for action, it's a mistake. Sit this dance out.

Change in the third line: Feeling the impulse in your thighs. Chasing after your following. Running on the merry-go-round will soon make you dizzy.

Like a politician who confuses a constituency for a conscience, you have located your purpose in the whims of those who look to you for leadership. This is untenable. It will lead you into confusion, vacillation and humiliation. Take stock of yourself. Since you have already set things powerfully in motion, it will require great strength and discipline to apply the brakes, but it is imperative that you do so.

Change in the fourth line: The influence of the heart. Wavering thoughts. A simple expression of intent gathers a true following.

You have a genuine purpose to which you are deeply connected. Second and third thoughts creep in, because you feel the need to consider a multitude of options and possibilities. This is natural but not optimal. Commit to your central idea, and those who share your commitment will be drawn to you.

Change in the fifth line: Feeling the influence in the back of the neck. It spreads to the tips of your fingers.

This influence stems from the deepest and most centered kind of cognition. Holistic thinking originates from and influences the body-mind in ways that accord with the highest principles of feeling, thought and will. When you proceed in such a way, you will not err.

Change in the top line: Influence of the jaws, cheeks and tongue. A fountain of wind.

Your commitment inspires you to hold forth in impassioned speech. There is nothing wrong with this. The right words at the right time can have a powerful emotional impact, but keep in mind that all they truly stir up is the atmosphere.

32

Endurance

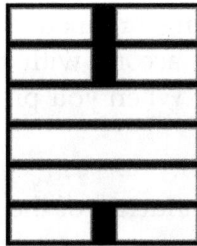

*Two things endure: the wind, because it
always has a direction to go; and
thunder, because it never ceases to
amaze.*

Associated concepts, images and attributes: Constancy, consistency, continuation, stamina, permanence, long-term enterprise or commitment, marriage, renewability, sustainability.

The Trigrams: Wind and Motion give rise to the image of a long-distance runner.

A living organism continually renews itself through the repetitive processes of inhalation and exhalation, systole and diastole, waking and sleeping, working and playing. It is this kind of endurance that is imaged here—not the endurance of inert material but of a living system which, like the partnership of a vital and sustainable marriage, remains in a constant state of adjustment and adaptation within a well-governed routine.

You are encouraged to keep to a regular schedule, to maintain or establish a healthy routine, to manage your life through habits that enhance your quality and enjoyment of life.

Changing Lines

Change in the first line: You jump in and take a knee. You are already over your head.

This is like making a marriage proposal on the first date. You want to go deep and establish a permanent connection before you even understand the situation or your role in it, much less the other parties involved. Hold your horses! Go slow! Take baby steps.

Change in the second line: Like a gyroscope. Remorse disappears.

The power and stability of a gyroscope keep it centered and self-correcting. You have established a process or a philosophy that will orient and sustain you for the long haul.

Change in the third line: Receiving an award, you blush and stammer. You don't keep your heart steady.

Something comes your way that ought to make you happy and proud, but feelings of shame and unworthiness undermine the experience, because in your heart, you have failed to honor your commitments and to keep faith with yourself. This is an intolerable situation. You simply have to do better than this.

Change in the fourth line: There is no game in the field.

Persistence for its own sake is pointless. You keep doing the same thing and hoping for a different result. You are stalking game that isn't there.

Change in the fifth line: Commitment to self-actualization. A gentle, inwardly adaptable approach is successful; constantly trying to manage it fails.

With regard to the care and feeding of the soul, one's feminine nature is better equipped than the more typically masculine qualities of order, control and strict adherence to duty, regardless of the gender of the person in question.

Change in the top line: A constant state of restlessness and agitation accomplishes nothing fast.

The relaxed mind works best because it is flexible enough to take in relevant information without rushing to conclusions. No matter how much you have to do or how little time you have in which to get it done, rushing around furiously is counter-productive. Life is too short. Take a break. Create a routine that allows time and space for regular periods of doing nothing at all, and you will become more productive.

33

Retreat

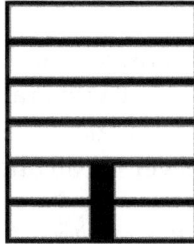

*An uphill retreat affords the opportunity
for a downhill battle.*

Associated concepts, images and attributes: Retreat, retirement, removal, withdrawal, seclusion, solitude, obscurity.

The Trigrams: Mountain and Sky give rise to the image of a mountain retreat or sanctuary.

Properly understood and executed, retreat becomes an important strategy for long-term success. Just as a tree drops its leaves at the onset of winter, and animals either withdraw into hibernation or migrate to more agreeable climates, when we follow the natural cycle of advance and retreat, we can avoid costly mistakes that drain us of energy, cut us off from our resources and leave us vulnerable to attack.

Overreaching works against you now. So does reacting to a threat by going on the offensive. Instead, you are encouraged to withdraw from your current position in order to give yourself a buffer against intrusion or interference. Avoid being drawn into a position of weakness or imbalance. Removing yourself from the situation in question does not mean abandoning your plans, but it will afford you a much needed opportunity to recuperate, reorganize your thoughts and recalibrate your tools, so that you might act decisively at the moment of your choosing. Do not let yourself be drawn into a fight (or even an opportunity) just now.

Changing Lines

Change in the first line: At the tail end of the retreat.

Caught in a web of obligations, you are the last to withdraw from danger and therefore the most vulnerable. The only thing to do under such circumstances is to take cover, keeping absolutely still and doing nothing whatsoever to call attention to yourself.

Change in the second line: Fighting back to back and tied together by a golden cord. You can't be torn away.

A gold cord symbolizes loyalty, obligation and duty as well as a centered connection to one's strength of character and inner purpose. In a time of retreat, you are powerfully connected to another person or to a principle that you cannot abandon. Nor will you be abandoned. Although your moral fiber may be severely tested, your faith in this relationship is absolute.

Change in the third line: Tied to the victims, you cannot escape alone. Enlist the support of soldiers and entertainers alike.

At a time when retreat is the only option, you are hamstrung by human relationships—specifically by a responsibility to those who will suffer most while others are removed to safety. You can't just cut and run, and you lack sufficient power to save those to whom you are obligated. The way out of such a dilemma is to enlist the support of those who are, in turn, obligated to you. Call on people who can execute your plans efficiently (your soldiers) and on those who can calm everybody's nerves in a time of crisis (your entertainers).

Change in the fourth line: Understanding comes in the wake of a gracious withdrawal. The small-minded impede you.

You can remove yourself from this affair with equanimity and grace, treating everyone kindly. But keep in mind that those who flatter and cajole you hope to keep you engaged for their benefit, not yours. Contrary to the previous line, where calling in favors might be necessary, here unsolicited help is available, but you don't need it and are counseled against accepting it.

Change in the fifth line: Honorable withdrawal. Appropriate and wise.

Here, withdrawal or retirement from a sphere of activity represents a kind of culmination. You have the capacity to move on to the next phase or project with dignity and self-respect, entirely free of hindrances and entanglements.

Change in the top line: Retreat brings you into abundance and generosity.

Leaving the turmoil of life behind, you find an unshakable inner contentment and appreciation for life that serves as the bedrock upon which true wealth and happiness stand unmolested. You enter a time of great fertility and enjoyment that will benefit you and everyone around you.

34

Use of Force

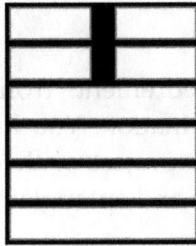

*Power corrupts those that it first
enslaves. By wielding more power than
an occasion requires, one loses mastery
of it; by losing mastery of it, one
becomes its slave.*

Associated concepts, images and attributes: Overwhelming
strength; personal power; charisma; invigorated and invigorating;
imbued with great ability, including the ability to cause harm or
injury.

The Trigrams: Sky and Movement suggest an image of the
legendary Thunderbird, credited with stirring up wind and storm
with the thunderous clap of its wings and with creating sheet
lightning with the blinding flash of its eyes.

Enormous power is available to you in this situation. So much so that, if wielded excessively or imprudently, the capacity for greatness can create more injury than good. Because the strength of your will, ideas and personality has surpassed that of any obstacles you might encounter, it is a good time to undertake something. It is not a good time, however, to blaze a path through uncharted territory. When General Tecumseh Sherman of the Union Army cut a swath through the South, burning crops and cutting Atlanta off from the rest of the Confederacy, he used this kind of strength to weaken his enemy and hasten the end of the Civil War. When President Truman gave the order to drop atomic bombs on Hiroshima and Nagasaki, this kind of force carried the day and ended World War II. Both men left legacies of supremacy and destruction. Both have been praised and both have been vilified.

Whatever you do now is likely to succeed. The same could be said of a bull in a china shop, depending on how one defines success. Be careful that you do no violence to your ideals.

Changing Lines

Change in the first line: A forced march leads into a trap. Misfortune is guaranteed.

You want to advance as rapidly as possible, but this is a mistake. You expend your power prematurely and risk harm to those who serve you. Avoid the temptation to have your way in the beginning, if you hope to continue.

Change in the second line: Wisdom advances. Your will emanates from the heart.

Because you are centered in your purpose and wise in your execution, you will avoid excess and achieve an unequivocal success.

Change in the third line: Headstrong, you can't retreat. You'll only get your horns caught in a fence.

You want to use force to break through a barrier. You use the weapons of your mind to try to browbeat your opposition, but the only way to avoid a disabling entanglement is not to use aggression in the first place. There are forces at work that are linked together in ways that you don't understand yet, so hold off on your attack. Keep your opinions in check.

Change in the fourth line: Fortunately, there's an opening in the fence, wide enough to drive a tractor-trailer through.

Opposition melts away. The intrigues and alliances that might have held you back simply fall apart. You can make great progress now.

Change in the fifth line: Dropping off a herd of goats. Afterwards, you can make easy progress. Shift gears and go.

Leaving behind a stubborn way of doing things will take a load off your mind and allow you to move forward with a lighter heart. Make the change. Use the strength of your imagination to find an easier way to go about things than charging headlong into every obstacle. Life gets a lot more interesting and enjoyable when you lighten up.

Change in the top line: The billy goat is caught in the fence again. Can't go forward, can't back up. It's going to take a lot of patience and muscle to get him unstuck.

Stubborn insistence on having your own way has led you into a difficult predicament. The only way out is to patiently correct each error individually. This might mean that you have amends to make with those you have offended or injured. The more you resist, the more difficult you make your own rescue, but if you can get through this, things will quickly turn around and the going will get easier.

35

Rising

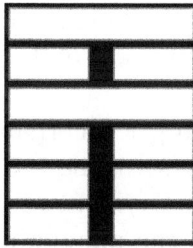

*The odds of finding a place in the sun
begin to improve when you get out of
bed in the morning.*

Associated concepts, images and attributes: Advance, prosperity, progress, flourishing, increasing in power, influence, optimism, a new day, the morning.

The Trigrams: Earth and Fire suggest an image of the rising sun, signifying a time of warmth, light and nourishing energy.

Ideas of progression, of making one's way in life or advancing ones ideas are suggested, as is the notion of sharing one's optimism and good fortune with others. Your influence extends in every direction now, among your peers and subordinates and also among those of even greater power, influence and ability. People of all walks of life are willing to listen to you, and you have the backing of your higher power or spiritual sources. Maintain your poise and confidence. Great things are possible.

Changing Lines

Change in the first line: Early to rise, but held in check. Your bootstraps are connected to a spiritual authority.

People feel threatened by your early success and would like to impede your progress. It might feel like you are going it alone, but in fact, you have an important network of alliances that have your best interests at heart. They recognize your gifts and respond accordingly. This experience will enrich you.

Change in the second line: Sunrise and rainfall. Sorrow woven with gladness. Accept the support of the goddess.

Your success is laced with grief. Perhaps, in your rise, you have had to leave something or someone behind. Don't let your losses hold you back from the enjoyment of your legitimate gains. By acknowledging both, you can allow a certain maternal influence to support you, bringing a wisdom and richness to your experience that is not to be had in any other way.

Change in the third line: The throng is with you. Rise up!

Everything is in order. You have the support you need. Give of yourself without hesitation. You will not regret it.

Change in the fourth line: Rising up like a rat; looking out for an opportunity, finding shame and danger.

Furtively seeking a private advantage or trying to work an angle, you will end up exposed and despised. This is not the way to proceed. Instead, step boldly into the light of day; state your case; own your intention.

Change in the fifth line: The earth turns to face the sun, not the sun to face the earth. The sun shines on without regret and without regard for up or down, morning or evening.

Real progress can no more be measured by opinion polls or profit margins than the output of the sun can be measured by the light that falls on the earth on a given day, since such measurements are affected by weather, time of day or seasonal angle. Similarly, the light you shed – which is to say, the good you do – is not dependent upon how it is received. Shine on! Keep doing what you do. Eventually the world will turn of its own accord to greet you, and it will just as surely turn away from you again. That is the nature of public attention. You follow your own nature.

Change in the top line: Take the bull by the horns and hold on tight. Recklessness is your downfall.

This is a situation in which you can power your way through any obstacle, but you must manage that power wisely if you want to advance your agenda. If it gets out of your control, it will embarrass you, and you will suffer the cost.

36

Night Vision

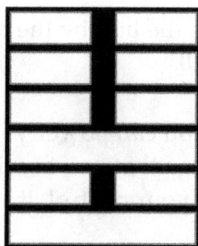

When caught in the light, most owls
seem rather more clownish than wise:
staring wide-eyed this way and
that. But they see what's going on
under cover of darkness, and because
they move without giving themselves
away, they can strike suddenly with
great effectiveness.

Associated concepts, images and attributes: Concealment, covering, camouflage, secrecy, protection, wounds, difficulty, destruction. Hidden worth.

The Trigrams: Fire and Earth give rise to images of nightfall, a banked fire, a shielded light.

When repressive or evil conditions prevail, often the best one can do is to carry on in secret, caring for those in danger and providing cover for the ongoing work of rescue. Examples in American history have included but have not been limited to the witch trials in colonial Massachusetts, the institution of slavery, the genocide of native populations, and the erosion of civil liberties during the McCarthy era and in the wake of the terrorist attacks at the turn of the 21st Century.

On a smaller scale, abusive or bullying conditions within a family, a school, a gang or, in fact, any social group might also indicate that one should work against the grain without wavering but also without heedlessly calling attention to oneself in ways that would only endanger one's cause.

In terms of personal development, it is sometimes necessary to acknowledge that the mind, when it has internalized abusive belief systems, can overpower the heart, the spirit and the will. It is important, under such conditions, to work diligently to protect the vulnerable desires and aspirations that one harbors in secret and to fortify them against self-criticism and self-sabotage. The ultimate aim, however, is always to work in the direction of a time when greater openness, sincerity and liberty can return.

Changing Lines

Change in the first line: "Swing low, Sweet Chariot, coming for to carry me home." ~ Wallis Willis

African-American spirituals, which often contained coded messages intended for the ears of runaway slaves, offer a clue to the kind of behavior that will serve you now. Keep your head down and your wits about you as you work to get out of an impossible situation. Know who to trust and who to avoid.

Change in the second line: Thrown, injured. Get back in the saddle and ride to the rescue.

The implication here is that, in striving to correct an oppressive situation, you face powerful opposition and a very real likelihood of serious injury to yourself and to your plans. Nevertheless, you have an opportunity to make a change that is greater than your sacrifice. If you choose to come to the rescue, you will need courage, imagination and an unflinching will.

Change in the third line: "No one can terrorize a whole nation, unless we are all his accomplices." ~Edward R. Murrow

During the "Red Scare" of the 1950s, newsman Edward R. Murrow exposed the bullying tactics of Senator Joseph McCarthy by airing in public what others had been too afraid to say. The lesson is clear: darkness cannot overwhelm the light, unless the light is extinguished. You can resolve the problem only by resolutely admitting the truth of your own observation.

Change in the fourth line: A blow to the gut. You get to the heart of the matter, but you can't stay where you are. Leave by the front door.

You may be shocked by the discovery of a secret agenda or hidden motive. Let the disturbance shake you loose from any questionable affiliations. You can no longer pretend that this is the place for you. Get out while you still can.

Change in the fifth line: The fictions of a spy serve to uncover the truth.

When no other possibility exists, you must pretend to be part of a bad situation by disguising your personal truth and playing along. This is a dangerous game, and it cuts you off from those upon whom you might otherwise rely. If you can maintain your own integrity, however, you will not only survive, you will gain invaluable intelligence and insight.

Change in the top line: What goes up must come down. The lights of heaven plummet to earth.

Here at the top of the hexagram, a point of climax is reached. Evil, being meteoric, must eventually burn itself out. That which has been in ascendance will soon fall of its own accord. Then the work of renovation can begin.

37

Family

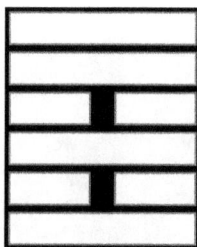

A family without discipline is like a
house without walls. If only the outside
elements would cooperate!

Associated concepts, images and attributes: Home, house, dwelling, household, familial roles, domesticity, enclosure, shelter, nesting.

The Trigrams: Wood and Fire give rise to the image of a roof overhead and a warm hearth below.

The family, regardless of its structure, represents a basic model for relationship and interaction in the larger world. It also provides a place of rest and shelter from the storms of life, not because it eliminates all need for competition, but because it harmonizes the more aggressive drives with a counterbalancing emphasis on cooperation. Discipline and flexibility are equally important, but a nurturing attitude reigns at the heart of all familial obligation.

You are asked to consider the roles you assume among the people with whom you live and work most closely and interdependently. Pay attention to the nesting and nurturing instincts that come into play or need to be expressed in your current situation. Provide what is needed now in terms of care and guidance.

Changing Lines

Change in the first line: Close the door firmly. Trouble disappears.

A paired meaning is suggested here. On the one hand, you may need to turn your attention away from the outside world in order to deal with matters closer to home. Something in the situation you face needs the security to be found in limiting options, or closing doors, and imposing strictures. At the same time, closing out the world allows one the opportunity to restore intimacy and to recharge one's batteries.

Change in the second line: At home in the kitchen. The only agenda is serving food.

Do not burden the situation with ulterior motives. You need only concern yourself with helping and nourishing those you care about. This locates you firmly in the center of things, just as the kitchen often serves as the real hub of activity in the home.

Change in the third line: Cutting words: if the wounds can be healed, all goes well in the end. Laughing words: if nothing is done about it, it leads to distress.

A balance needs to be struck between stern severity and over-indulgence. In bringing up a child, it is better to err on the side of discipline than laxity. In a marital or parent-child relationship, a fight can clear the air and lead to honest reconciliation, whereas insolence and mockery only make matters worse. In looking at your current dilemma, consider how you might apply the lessons of sound parenting. Harsh measures must be implemented with fairness, but over-indulgence is harder to correct.

Change in the fourth line: Wealth and generosity dwell here.

This is an auspicious time and place. Make the most of it. Be generous and loving in your relationships, and you will prosper even more from your connections.

Change in the fifth line: Imagination governs the heart without fear. Mingling in mutual affection inspires trust.

The world around you is a reflection of your own nature. Look upon it with kindness, and it will return your gaze. Continue with your most benevolent plans. You have the support of kindred spirits.

Change in the top line: You make a lasting impression. The support of a hundred kindred spirits is good for a lifetime.

The individual is identified here as the head of a family, one who has earned great respect through selfless service over the course of time. With this backing comes the ability to act on your desires. You will accomplish whatever you set out to do.

38

Polarization

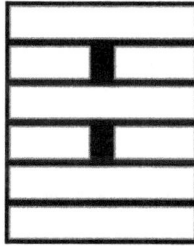

*My enemy is my mirror, his left my
right, his vice my virtue.*

Associated concepts, images and attributes: Separation,
segregation, opposition, polarization, divisiveness, divergence,
diversity, exclusivity, animosity, anger, isolation, alienation,
repulsion, demonization.

The Trigrams: Lake and Fire suggest a tendency toward
polarization and, at the same time, a mirroring of opposites like a
torch in a reflecting pool.

In general, when factions subject to divergent aims or tendencies
form within a larger group, cooperative effort stalls and the
achievement of any goal is made more difficult. The story of the
Tower of Babel serves as a familiar biblical example, as do many
episodes in American history, from the Civil War to the unrest of
the 1960's and the divisive rhetoric of fringe politics in any era. In

the individual, the same pattern shows itself in feelings of alienation or scatteredness.

It is also true that opposites attract. Isolation can serve as the prelude to individual growth and development that is necessary for union or synthesis. We see this in cell division and replication, in the preadolescent tendency to shun the opposite sex, in many forms of specialization, in constructive debate and political compromise, and in the renewal and intensification of intimacy following the resolution of a domestic dispute.

Within the prevailing atmosphere of disunion or alienation, you are encouraged to recognize opportunities for connection and reunion. They are present and can serve as guideposts to get you through a lonely, difficult and even dangerous time.

Changing Lines

Change in the first line: Sorrows dissipate. If you lose your horse, don't chase it. If you see repulsive people, eliminate blame.

The more you try to grasp an idea, the more elusive it becomes. The more you try to prove a point, the more people shy away from you or turn a deaf ear. The more fault you find in the other person's point of view, the more you remove yourself from the dialog. Be still. Do nothing. What is truly relevant to you in the situation will return to be with you. What does not concern you will evaporate.

Change in the second line: Down a crooked road, you meet the one who will be straight with you.

An unexpected turn of events puts you in touch with something or someone who possesses the power to reorganize your thinking, making things readily apparent that have been hidden from your view. Recognize the opportunity and embrace it. It will change you for the better.

Change in the third line: You see your car jacked and your body pulled from it, your limbs broken, your nose cut off. No way to set out, no way to end up.

Your plans will not come to fruition. You will be soundly defeated and lose face in the bargain. A clue to your survival is given in the perspective presented here. You can witness what happens, or will happen, as if from a distance. If you have not yet set things in motion, be forewarned. The opposition you will encounter is simply too great for you to handle.

Change in the fourth line: Going your own way, you meet your mate in the form of a spirit animal or guide.

The changing fourth line presents the idea of isolation, whether voluntary or enforced, as a shamanistic quest or journey, not unlike the vision quest of aboriginal Americans or the walkabout of aboriginal Australians. In any case, you march to the beat of your own drum and, in the process, encounter a primal force to which you feel powerfully attracted. This power belongs with you, is part of you, will guide and partner with you from now on.

Change in the fifth line: In the darkness, the bite of a totem animal breaks the skin. How is this a bad thing?

In the fourth line, the animal spirit is a personal guide that belongs with you and you alone. Here it represents a totem, or ancestral spirit, that comes to you during a time of estrangement and bites through the barrier of self-containment, or identity, that separates you from the world of spiritual kinship. This is frightening, of course, but also transformative.

Change in the top line: A prodigal son sees himself surrounded by filthy pigs. He takes up an axe, then sets it aside. Faces come out of the rain.

Feeling isolated, cut off from familiar sources of support, you see the world through dung-colored glasses. But if you can bring yourself to set aside your animosity, you will see that the people

123

who approach you now are not your enemies. Tears of regret, like rain, will wash your vision clear, and you will see people for who they are. Join with them. Treat them as family. This will return you to your senses, including your sense of identity and self-esteem.

39

Impediment

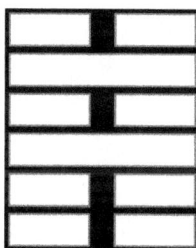

A boulder does not block a path, it only
moves the path to one side.

Associated concepts, images and attributes: Obstruction,
blockage, interruption, affliction, difficulty, weakness, disability.

The Trigrams: Mountain and Water give rise to the image of a
mountain pass closed with snow and ice.

The situation described here cannot be faced head-on or in the
usual way. The first option worth considering is to wait, to pull
back until the situation resolves itself or until you are able to re-
imagine the predicament, to see it in a new way and proceed in a
different direction. In this way, you reserve your strength instead
of wasting it. Your goal may seem more distant than ever,
particularly if you withdraw from the obstruction in defeat. The
solution lies not in isolation but in collaboration with others who
have experienced similar problems and have overcome them.

Allow difficulty to strengthen your resolve, not weaken it. Use a time of delay to develop your imagination and flexibility.

Changing Lines

Change in the first line: The way forward invites complication. The way back invites compliments.

Resist the temptation to plow your way through. This will only compound the problem and deprive you of strength. Instead, pull back. Keep an open mind and a soft focus, allowing new impressions to enter into your consideration. If you can exercise patience and imagination, your restraint and wisdom will not go unnoticed.

Change in the second line: A noble slave. Toil and trouble are your lot but not your fault.

You serve a purpose higher than yourself, and in this instance the difficulty cannot be avoided. You will have to work your way through the obstacle, not around it, regardless of the drudgery and personal risk involved. You may not be responsible for the problem, but you are responsible for the solution.

Change in the third line: The way there invites danger. The way home invites celebration.

Your duty is not to face down this difficulty or danger but, in fact, to turn away from it. Someone or something important to you will be exposed to danger if you continue to force your way through the obstacles. Sometimes, being a hero means standing down.

Change in the fourth line: The way forward is blocked. The way back develops character and the will to continue.

Going on alone is not the solution. You will only beat your head against a mounting wall of opposition. If, instead, you can hold off until help arrives, you will find your way through the difficulties with the help of others who see the value in helping you to accomplish your goal.

Change in the fifth line: Trouble everywhere. Partners are coming. Organize them.

You may feel overwhelmed and want to give up, but don't. Help is on the way. Your job is to be clear about the nature of the problem, what needs to be done and what roles need to be filled.

Change in the top line: You attend a school of hard knocks, but the apple on your desk is sweet. Cross the threshold and gain a following.

The ripeness of the apple represents the fullness of the desire to learn, to devour life and wisdom alike. That desire contains the seeds of the future. Here, impediments in life become the pediment over the door to a school. Your difficulties have been your best and greatest teachers. It may be that you are in a position now to pass on to others the lessons gained by your own experience. If so, remember how much you yourself have learned directly, not from admonition but from adversity and adventure.

40

Release

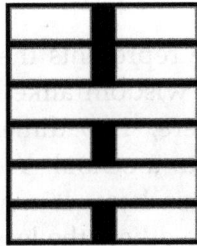

*A free hand is able to grasp, but a
grasping hand is not free.*

Associated concepts, images and attributes: Loosening, untying, deliverance, scattering, releasing, dispelling.

The Trigrams: Water and Movement imply the sudden release of tension or pent up energy as in a thunderstorm or a dam burst.

A threat has been eliminated or resolved, a source of concern neutralized, or an inhibition removed. The resulting release of tension delivers you from fear, obstruction and isolation. Shake off the effects of it. If there are no residual matters to be cleared up, things should be allowed to return to normal, and you can go about your business once again. If residual elements of the situation require further attention, it would be wise to see to them sooner rather than later.

Changing Lines

Change in the first line: No harm, no foul.

There's really nothing to discuss. You've done nothing wrong. You are right where you need to be, doing what you need to do. Carry on.

Change in the second line: Three fine foxes in a field. Take them down with a single arrow.

Through sincerity and directness, you can disable the cunning of adversaries, flatterers and false friends, acquiring thereby the intelligence, skill and power you need to carry out your aims.

Change in the third line: Carrying a backpack, hitching a ride in a limousine. You're just so gangsta!

Being needy, you accept the favors of powerful people and try to act like a big shot yourself. This influence will corrupt you. Shake it off while you still can.

Change in the fourth line: Loosen your grasp. Then you can shake hands with your friends.

You are attached to someone or something you think you need, but there is no real connection there. When you let go, you may find yourself alone and empty-handed at first, but those who truly believe in you and in what you stand for will be free to return and to lend their support.

Change in the fifth line: Shake off the reins; hold fast to your spiritual connection. Your handlers will withdraw.

You have been manipulated by a sense of obligation to the needs of others, but this interferes with your true purpose. Shake loose of them and follow your heart's desire. Don't worry, when self-interested people see that you no longer serve them, they will find another horse to ride.

Change in the top line: A hawk perched on a high wall. Your aim is good. Take it down.

Something predatory occupies a position of authority and restricts your freedom of thought, expression or movement. It must be removed. Attack it now.

41

Reduction

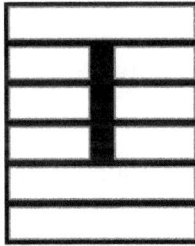

Less is more when it whets the appetite.

Associated concepts, images and attributes: Reduction, decrease, subtraction, minimization, concentration, simplification, suppression, sacrifice.

The Trigrams: Metal and Stone give rise to the image of a blade held against a grindstone.

The elimination of excess is an important principle in the ongoing process of change, growth and development. The structure of the hexagram is such that the strong lines at the bottom, tending to rise, sacrifice themselves to the receptive lines stationed above them. We see the principle of decrease at work in bringing a fine edge to a blade to increase its effectiveness. The forcible collection of taxes as well as voluntary giving to charitable causes are also examples of reduction. We put the energy of decrease to use in paying bills, cleaning house or clearing a desk of clutter, in dieting or weeding a garden or setting aside time for meditation, exercise or religious observance. Since matter and energy can be neither created nor destroyed, decrease in one area necessarily brings about increase in another, and vice versa.

The advice given here is to reduce something in the current situation that has grown excessive or outmoded. Eliminate one thing in order to make room for something else. Simplify your involvement. Do less, say less. Reduce your expectations. Make an offering or sacrifice to something greater than yourself. This is not to be done on blind faith but with a clear understanding of the need and purpose behind the decrease. Question your motives and also the motives of those who stand to benefit from your loss.

You may well experience pain, loss or injury as a result of giving something up, but if the effort is made as an expression of appreciation and gratitude for abundance, the benefits will outweigh the harm. Begrudging the loss will defeat your purpose.

Changing Lines

Change in the first line: Bring the matter to a head, expunge it and move on quickly. Talk it out.

The excess here takes the form of something purulent or toxic that must be eliminated before it causes real harm. Treat it as you would an abscess by bringing it to the surface where it can be discussed openly and honestly. Once the matter is resolved, go about your business and do not revisit it.

Change in the second line: Put it to the test and realize the benefit. Don't try to correct it or diminish it in any way; instead, augment it.

Contrary to the general meaning of the hexagram, the situation in the second line is wholly advantageous and should not be tampered with or hindered in any way. Quite the opposite, in fact. Do what you can to encourage it.

Change in the third line: The trio loses a player. The solo soon becomes a duet.

In peer relationships, the triangle is the least stable arrangement. If you are feeling like the odd one out, you would probably be better served by going your own way for the time being, since it opens the way for a more viable partnership down the road. If you are in a partnership that you value, the advice is to reduce the occasion for jealousy.

Change in the fourth line: Eliminate the affliction. Send a messenger. Then you can celebrate.

Your attachment to something or someone is doing you real harm. Sever ties immediately. The use of an intermediary — that is, an uninvolved third party — leaves no opening for negotiation and makes the break cleaner. You will enjoy the relief that disentanglement brings.

Change in the fifth line: Someone must be throwing the switches for you. Green lights all the way.

It is as if a divine hand has cleared the way for you, eliminating every obstacle in your path. You can make uninhibited progress now.

Change in the top line: No decrease at all, nor any blame attached to the increase. Take this show on the road. You have an entourage but no place to call home.

Here at the top of the hexagram, you occupy the position of recipient, the one to whom others extend their collective trust and power. This is not a time to relax, however, since you are, in effect, a public servant. You have all the help you need, but that doesn't mean that you get to sit back and reap the benefits, because the cycle of increase and decrease must continue. If you treat these newfound resources as your private property, they will quickly evaporate.

42

Replication

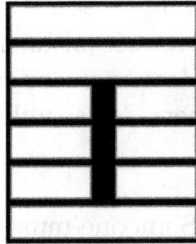

If it's working, don't fix it, replicate it!

Associated concepts, images and attributes: Advance, growth and development, fertility, promotion, reinvestment, increased effort or input.

The Trigrams: Movement and Penetration give rise to images of copulation and fertility rites.

In a reversal of the trend in the previous hexagram (Reduction), here a sacrifice on the part of the higher element reinforces the lower, or root, element to stimulate, arouse and impregnate. In spiritual and economic terms alike, the resulting stimulus benefits every level of interaction.

You are encouraged to invest the resources at your disposal, to pour more in, to promote the growth and development of an idea, a relationship, a project or a business, to increase your involvement or commitment. This new influx of energy will lead to success. It is a good time to set out on a new project.

Changing Lines

Change in the first line: Use the increase to accomplish something great. The way is open. This is not a mistake.

Great resources have been placed at your disposal for a reason. Organize them, draw up a plan and apply them where they can do the greatest good that you can imagine. You will succeed.

Change in the second line: Someone must be throwing the switches for you. Green lights ahead for as far as the eye can see.

It is as if a divine hand has cleared the way for you, eliminating every obstacle. You can make uninhibited progress now and in the future. Maintain your connection to this positive flow, and anything you want to do will succeed.

Change in the third line: Make good use of the setback. The balance of power is shifting. Move with the center and speak to the one in charge.

Along with increase comes disruption. This may strike you as unfortunate at first, but if you can adapt to the changes, it will turn out to your advantage. Insist on your right of access to those who are at the forefront of the innovation.

Change in the fourth line: The balance of power is shifting. Notify the one in charge. Maintain loyalties and move with the changes.

You are in a position to see major changes coming before it becomes apparent to those in power. With this knowledge comes the responsibility to warn them and to do what you can to enable a smooth and beneficial transition. Your loyalties may be tested. Act with determination.

Change in the fifth line: You proceed from a kind and benevolent heart. There is no question.

The response to the question of your heart is an unqualified yes! When you are guided by the most basic instincts of love and human kindness, there is no basis for doubt. Follow your desire.

Change in the top line: Whose coffers are you lining? Your assassin's? Look in your heart for the reason.

What you contemplate is self-serving and luxury-seeking. It will enrage your enemies and make it easy for them to remove you from a position of authority. You may be tempted to blame outside forces for your demise, but that misses the point entirely. You are in need of serious self-examination.

43

Parting Company

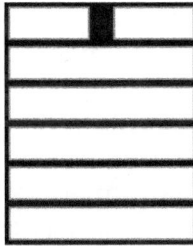

The difference between the path you take
and the company you keep is a subtle
one.

Associated concepts, images and attributes: A parting of the ways, a fork in the road, breaking up, separation, divorce, severance, resignation or termination, end of a relationship.

The Trigrams: Initiative and Metal suggest the image of a blade used to cleave or separate a whole into two halves.

The general recommendation, when one faces the difficult task of parting company, is to take resolute action, to make one's intention known and to set off in the direction of one's individual purpose with confident strides. Make an announcement. This is a public, not a private, matter. Since the termination of a single significant relationship impacts the wider social network, it is vital that you inform everyone involved.

Often, when one terminates a relationship, the other party will seek to re-engage by going on the offensive. It is a mistake to respond to attacks by defending one's position, since by definition, such a position has already been abandoned. Move on. If there is nothing left to improve on, then there is nothing left to prove. Set new goals for yourself and actively pursue them.

Changing Lines

Change in the first line: Leaping to get away. Uncoordinated running trips you up.

Acting impulsively, without a plan, will backfire. Take small, manageable steps in the beginning. The resistance you face— whether internal or external—is too great to make a complete break. Bide your time.

Change in the second line: Red flags, alarm bells ringing. Sleepless nights with a gun under the pillow. No time for fear.

The situation is tense. It keeps you on edge, but in this there is a certain exhilaration. Don't worry about that; adrenaline serves you now. Keep your wits about you and you won't succumb to the senselessness of outright fear.

Change in the third line: The cheeky one engages and gets caught in a trap. Mud washes off your name more easily when your own hands are clean.

Hurling insults and criticism back and forth keeps you engaged in an unhealthy pattern of relationship. No matter how justified it may seem, retribution is far more dangerous than simply turning your back and going your own way. Though you suffer the indignity of gossip and public ridicule, that is preferable to indulging in it yourself.

Change in the fourth line: Limping away to a new camp with a mule in tow. Sorrows disappear. The news is unreliable.

Wounded in relationship, it has become necessary to move to a new place where you can rest and recuperate. This requires a stubborn determination, overcoming a great reluctance to move forward. Once you complete the transition, you will find relief, not regret. However, because you have distanced yourself from your usual sources of information or because you now know those sources to have been suspect all along, you will not be able to trust everything you hear.

Change in the fifth line: Through the swamp or over the mountain? You can do no wrong, because the heart takes a middle path.

The way parts. You have a clear choice to make and you must make it with conviction. You can take the high road or the low road, but not both at once; which way you go will decide the difficulties you face. Because you have an emotional connection to both courses of action, neither direction is inherently wrong for you. Whatever you decide, therefore, becomes the only thing to do. Don't look back.

Change in the top line: The alarm has been silenced. Disaster strikes.

Either you have been lulled into a false sense of security or you are more afraid of calling attention to an issue and getting the help you need than you are of the consequences of your own silence. Either way, you make grave mistake. Rouse yourself! There is no time to lose. Make noise! Draw attention to the problem before it destroys you and everything you care about!

44

Coupling

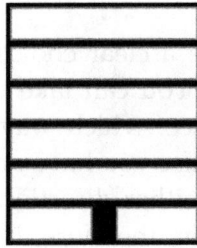

*The eagle is made for the wind, not the
wind for the eagle. The perpetuation of
an idea depends on knowing what it
means to get carried away.*

Associated concepts, images and attributes: Introduction, initiation, attraction, romance, temptation, seduction, copulation, engagement, marriage, proposal or proposition, merger, destiny, sexual and/or political intrigue, fertility. Emergence of the goddess or muse, the divine feminine, a powerful and fertile influence.

The Trigrams: Penetration and Initiative suggest seduction and a desire for powerful union.

The stirring of a powerful and attractive new element or influence makes itself felt. Its appearance may be sudden and may seem fleeting and inconsequential, but it augers a time of great fertility and continuation. We find ourselves in the grip of elemental forces that are beyond our power to grasp or to control. Regardless of the temptation, we are warned against trying to appropriate or co-opt this seductive energy to our own ends. It will command us, not the other way around.

Changing Lines

Change in the first line: Apply the brakes. If you try to steer, you'll end up in the ditch, spilling your cargo and disabling yourself in the bargain.

The raw power of attraction is enormous. You want to make use of a new influx of energy, but if you try, the forward momentum will prove too great to control. You cannot restrain it, but you can and must put a leash on your own designs. Be firm with yourself. Otherwise, you will lose the ability to act more effectively when things settle down again — as they will.

Change in the second line: A fetus in the womb. No harm in that, but it's not a good time to make announcements.

The situation is pregnant with hidden potential. As exciting or as distressing as this may be, you should keep the news to yourself for now. Seclusion is beneficial in order to allow the new influence to develop in its own way, without outside interference. Nurture it by nourishing yourself.

Change in the third line: Fatefully injured, limping away to a new bed. Haunted by it, you resist.

You have been wounded as a result of a brief but powerful encounter. While this makes it difficult to move in any direction, it is essential that you withdraw to a place of rest and recuperation. Unless and until you can deal effectively with what has happened, you will not be able to move forward.

Change in the fourth line: Coupling with an empty womb. An exercise in futility, not fertility.

There are no creative possibilities in this particular connection at the moment. No matter how tempting it might be to continue, you are wasting your time and deluding yourself if you expect anything to come of it.

Change in the fifth line: Ripe as a watermelon, she comes bearing a child of the gods.

This connection bears the stamp of a divine origin. A fortuitous new beginning is pregnant with possibilities. Like the birth of a child who will continue one's lineage, it promises to add meaning, purpose and beauty to your life.

Change in the top line: Coupling like a horny old goat. Exhausting, though not blameworthy.

Because you approach this connection as a test of your prowess, any deeper meaning or benefit is lost on you. While there is nothing terribly wrong in what you're doing, it is unfortunate in that it will deplete you of resources and deprive you of joys that you will not have known were possible.

45

Assembly

When the right people are assembled,
it's like water pooling in a lake;
everything is elevated – the mood, the
level of discourse, expectations and
possibilities. Many hands make light
work.

Associated concepts, images and attributes: Assembly, cluster, collection, throng, community, company, union, federation, association.

The Trigrams: Earth and Lake suggest the image of a valley where water collects in a natural basin.

A group has formed around a strong central purpose or a forceful and charismatic leader. With effective organization, each member finds a meaningful role and powerful expression. The energy of such a group is available and ought not to be wasted.

The task at hand is to organize individuals or smaller groups into a cohesive whole by making two things clear: the unifying principle or purpose of the larger group and each participant's role in the fulfillment of that purpose. The first step in this process is to organize one's own mind, to collect one's personal energies and to bring them into alignment with the overarching purpose of the group. Then you can reach out with confidence to effectively engage the energies of others. Great things are possible. Great devotion is required.

Changing Lines

Change in the first line: Deeply felt, but you haven't closed the deal. On again, off again. Make the call! Reach out and shake hands! Then you will infect them with your enthusiasm.

You know what you want to do, and you are committed to it. Let people know. Others are willing and ready to lend you their support. They are confused only by your reticence. As soon as you dispel their insecurities, the tension will evaporate, and everyone—including you—will be in for a pleasant surprise.

Change in the second line: Extend the network and the timeline. Stretch to accommodate greatness. Anticipate transformation.

What you are involved in is bigger than you have allowed yourself to envision. Go beyond the usual circles to include more people. Allow more time for things to develop. You will grow according to the scale of what's needed, and it will change you in ways that you have not yet imagined. Trust the process; have faith in the spirit that moves this group.

Change in the third line: Gathering at a funeral means tears. Climbing in the coffin to rouse the dead is a mistake. There's no harm in moving on to higher ground.

You feel an emotional attachment to a certain group and long to be more a part of it, but that doesn't mean that either the emotion or the group is right for you. You can't fix this. None of your plans around this situation are workable. You may have to mourn the loss of a cherished ideal, but when you accept the finality of things as they are and distance yourself from those who have moved on without you anyway, you will find support from a source that is more vital to you and for something to which you are better suited.

Change in the fourth line: Gathering excellence. You can do no wrong.

You are poised to do great things. Collect the energy around you and put it to good use.

Change in the fifth line: Gathering impeccable strength rejuvenates you again and again. Gathering in secret puts your purpose on a dimmer switch.

When you are equal to your tasks and have earned a position of authority, you can meet any challenge and will continue to do the important work around which the group is organized. If, on the other hand, you have gained a leadership position not by merit but in some other way, if the inherent power of such a position corrupts you or you use it to make secret deals, then the entire enterprise becomes suspect and its mission is diminished.

Change in the top line: Gathering at a funeral. Sobs, tears, snot. No problem.

You are united with others by a common grief or tragedy. There is nothing wrong with expressing your emotion. It is the right thing to do, it solidifies your bond and opens the lines of communication.

46

Climbing

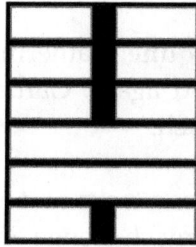

*The first step in climbing is to know the
reason for it. There is joy enough, for
some, in climbing for its own sake; for
others, in climbing to get to someplace
new or to get away from someplace old,
to improve the view, to face a challenge,
to say I told you so... In every case, the
climber meets resistance. Climbing
without resistance is just walking, and
for some, taking a level path seems
perfectly reasonable.*

Associated concepts, images and attributes: Upward mobility,
rags to riches, entrepreneurship, achievement, progress,
development.

The Trigrams: Wood and Earth suggests the image of a seedling, with the downward penetration of its root and the simultaneous pushing upward of its shoot through the soil to reach the light.

The "American Experiment" has uniquely intertwined two opposing forces: that of democracy, which seeks to provide a level playing field of equal rights and opportunities regardless of one's status at the time of birth; and capitalism, which favors the accumulation of personal wealth and the formation of socio-economic classes. The resulting tension in the social and political spheres is reflected in the individual's struggle to rise out of obscurity and inhibition and into an arena of public esteem by means of inner drive and purpose. Using the energy of upward mobility is not a matter of achieving meteoric success or "fifteen minutes of fame" (for that, see hexagram 30, line 4) but of remaining grounded enough to put in the patient and diligent effort required to build something of lasting value in the world. The more broadly that value is distributed, the more people you benefit, and the more lasting your accomplishment becomes.

Changing Lines

Change in the first line: Climbing sincerely. Tethered to someone above.

Your early efforts, because they serve something greater than yourself, attract the attention of those of a higher station, who recognize your value. (The first line occupies a position of correspondence to the fourth, both of which are firmly grounded.) This bodes well.

Change in the second line: Tethered to one's purpose, dedicated to climbing. No harm in a cheerful ascent.

Your inner drive and your connections in the outer world accord with one another. (The second line corresponds to the fifth.) It is right and good to make use of this influence to further your agenda, and no one can blame you for taking pleasure in your good fortune. Let it stimulate you to keep pushing onward and upward.

Change in the third line: Climbing through an open gate into an abandoned field. No doubt about it.

Resistance vanishes. Nothing and no one stands in your way. Having grown accustomed to struggle, you may be tempted to question such a sudden turn of events in your favor, but don't let it stop you. Make the most of it.

Change in the fourth line: Ascend to the peak. Take your place among the great ones in the hall of fame.

Your accomplishments will stand the test of time. If you make the effort now to provide something of merit and value to the common good, you will establish a durable connection to the greatness that you inherit from your spiritual forebears. The way forward stands open and unobstructed.

Change in the fifth line: Climbing the steps to the monument.

Your spiritual legacy is assured, provided you maintain a sobriety appropriate to the occasion and skip over none of the steps in the process. With humility, as expressed through diligent and sustained effort, come great honor and prestige.

Change in the top line: Climbing in the dark under a waning moon. No rest for the weary.

A lack of clarity about the situation makes progress both difficult and dangerous, but you can't stop now. Burn the midnight oil. Only persistent effort and due diligence will afford you an opportunity to clear things up.

47

Exhaustion

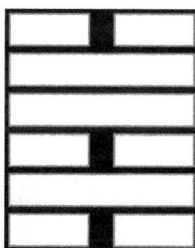

It is easy to gauge the depth of a dry
lake; it takes vision to see it filled again.

Associated concepts, images and attributes: Depletion of resources, the end of the road, oppression, solitary confinement, tribulation, cut off, thrown back on oneself, down on one's luck, a moment of truth.

The Trigrams: Water and Metal, with the water below and the metal (container) above suggest the image of a leaky bucket or a dry lakebed.

A period of suffering and deprivation is indicated, the resolution of which is wholly dependent on the courage, will and ingenuity of the sufferer. Help from the outside is either unavailable or ineffective. The City of New Orleans in the aftermath of Hurricane

Katrina serves as one example of such a depletion of resources, which may be accompanied by a feeling of abandonment.

Impoverished and circular logic traps us in a downward spiral of neediness and leakage of energy. Pleas for help, coming from one who has nothing to offer in return, are likely to fall on deaf ears. Regardless of one's responsibility or lack of it, blaming "the system" (or indeed any set of external conditions) without the energy required to renovate that system, is likewise an exercise in futility.

Extraordinary circumstances call for extraordinary patience, faith and creativity. When fate turns against us, when we are tested to the limits of our endurance, we are forced to take our own true measure. We must reach deeper than we know and venture outside the usual network of support if we wish to access a source of power and resilience that has no limits.

Changing Lines

Change in the first line: Slumped under a dead tree, wandering in a valley of shadows, you won't find anything worthwhile.

Adopting an attitude of defeat, dwelling on the past and what has gone wrong will only keep you trapped in your predicament. Even if an opportunity for improvement presents itself, in your current frame of mind, you won't recognize it. If you want to find a solution, the place to begin is with your body: adopt a smile, change your posture; walk with a sense of purpose and eventually you will find a purpose that makes sense.

Change in the second line: Eating and drinking. Exhausted, but your ship is coming in. Don't try to make sense of everything yet.

Here the state of oppression is primarily psychological. Your basic needs are met, though you are not fulfilled. Have a little patience and refrain from taking your personal dissatisfaction out on other people. Your luck is turning. In fact, new and more meaningful opportunities will soon be pouring in from all sides. You may find yourself overwhelmed by good fortune, but you are cautioned against trying to place artificial limits on things or choosing between them prematurely. They will sort themselves out soon enough.

Change in the third line: Turned to stone, grasping at vines and thorns. Closing the doors and drawing the blinds, you won't even see your partner.

You are your own worst enemy. By cutting yourself off from your emotions and engaging in self-injurious and addictive behaviors, you isolate yourself from the world at large and, even worse, from those who care more about you than you do yourself.

Change in the fourth line: Riding in a luxury sedan through downtown traffic, moving at a snail's pace and feeling hindered. Even so, you are in good company and making progress.

Things are not moving quickly enough for you. Delays result from the influences of others who have their own agendas and to whom you feel beholden. This is distressing, but don't give up on your own ideas. You will, in the end, accomplish what you set out to do.

Change in the fifth line: A black eye and two busted kneecaps, shambling along in leg irons. Setting the record straight unlocks them. Carry on.

You suffer a loss of face and are crippled in your efforts as a result of interference from someone in a position of authority. Since your purpose is worth defending, defend it truthfully. In the end, you will be freed of the obstruction, and you can put this episode behind you.

Change in the top line: Caught in a web of conspiracy theories. If you can get over yourself and get moving again, you'll have an easier time of it.

You imagine things to be much worse than they are, but consider whether your own sense of self-importance might be contributing to the problem. Stop looking for secret motives in everyone else, but don't be afraid to stir things up—particularly in yourself. In short, the recipe for change contains less speculation and more action.

48

The Well

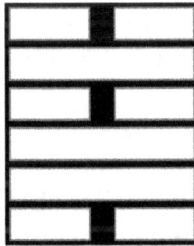

*The well of human wisdom is some
4,000 years deep and has yet to be
exhausted. It is replenished in every
generation at a rate that far exceeds its
use. So drink your fill! Bathe in it!
Irrigate your gardens and your
neighbors' gardens, too!*

Associated concepts, images and attributes: Communication, inspiration, motivation, shared resources via the social network and human forms of interaction via oral and written communication, art, literature, music, drama, etc.

The Trigrams: Wind and Water suggest the image of an old-fashioned windmill used to pump groundwater to the surface for everyday use.

A well is a man-made structure that taps into a deep, renewable source of life and makes it available for a variety of uses. The location and structure of a well can be changed, and so can the technology by which it operates, but the water in it remains the same as it has been since the creation of the earth. Two things are important about a well: its depth and its ability to bring water to the surface. If we look for inspiration in the superficial, if we fail to plumb the depths of our inter-connectedness with others, or if we are careless in the way we make these resources available, we are denied the nourishing benefits that we crave, and we can die of spiritual and cultural thirst.

You have the opportunity, perennially, to enrich the world in which you live, first by gaining access to primordial wisdom for yourself and then by making it available to others.

Changing Lines

Change in the first line: The well is choked with mud. No one can drink this water. Nothing wild comes to an unproductive well.

You want and need to get back to a primal source of inspiration and a sense of meaningful purpose, but nothing comes of it when you try. You need to dig deeper, to get back to your original "wild" nature. That means dredging up a lot of useless and obstructive material that has accumulated over time. You may need to get your hands dirty with work that you do for yourself and yourself alone.

Change in the second line: The water main is broken. It runs into a gulley where people go to catch fish.

Instead of providing for everyone, the usual channels of communication are neglected and have fallen into a state of disrepair. Good ideas and information go wasted. Those who have access to them only use them for their own gain, not for the common good. The problem is not the material itself but the manner in which it is transmitted or presented. Look to your method of delivery, your medium, or the manner in which you communicate your ideas. What can you do to make them more useful and more accessible?

Change in the third line: The water in the well is clear and sweet, but no one drinks it. It breaks my heart. If only the right person knew about it, everyone could partake.

You have something of value to share but no one with whom to share it. This is a sad and lonely situation, but it won't last forever. The "right person" is one who understands the merit of your ideas and possesses the magnetism to draw others to them as well. The line makes no promise that such a person will come along, but the suggestion is clear that the quality of your gift is such that, with the right sponsorship, it would have universal appeal.

Change in the fourth line: Lining the well means a little downtime, but it's all good.

This is a time of inner development and self-improvement. Such good and necessary work may seem to have little impact on the outer world, but that condition is only temporary. What you do now will make a difference in the quality of your service later on.

Change in the fifth line: Clear, cold water. Good to drink.

You have access to a source of deep and refreshing vitality that has the capacity to provide meaning and purpose to your life, your work and your society. The rest is up to you. Make use of it and give thanks.

Change in the top line: Drawing from an uncovered well. The supply is dependable. Good fortune all around.

There is no impediment to your good fortune. You have tapped into an inexhaustible supply of meaning and inspiration. Not only will it serve you copiously, there is enough to supply the entire community.

49

The Engine

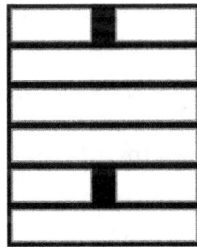

If you want to be the engine of change
the world, you need two things: a fire in
your belly and a joy in your heart. Only
when the fire down below has brought
things to a boil, can your revolution
build up enough steam to get moving.

Associated concepts, images and attributes: Radical change; renewal; reformation; removal; overthrow; overhaul; the reinvention or transformation of the self; a fundamental change of belief, role, or identity.

The Trigrams, Fire and Metal suggest the image of an engine — steam, electric, turbine, internal combustion or any other kind.

The introduction of the steam to power factories, locomotives and steamboats transformed not only the American landscape but every aspect of our society, industry and economy. The internal combustion engine redesigned everything again, from agriculture to architecture. Its effects are seen in highway design, city planning, pipelines, oil refineries and attached garages. The depletion of oil reserves have resulted in the appearance of wind farms and photovoltaic arrays. The means by which we harness and employ energy have changed fundamentally and repeatedly, and such transformations will continue to alter the course of our history. In every case, powerful influences have championed change, while others have impeded it.

In the life of the individual, the structures, habits and principles upon which one bases one's way of life are also subject to radical change. As composite beings with competing loyalties, ambitions and agendas, each of us must recognize the struggles that rage within us and understand that in matters of self-transformation, just as in the external world of political in-fighting, intrigue and upheaval, timing is crucial to the success of any radical undertaking. While such changes are recognized in the lines of the 49th hexagram as inevitable, the ill-timed or premature revolution is ill-fated. Knowing when to act is crucial.

Changing Lines

Change in the first line: Tied to your purpose. Not yet time to take action.

Your desire to instigate a change in the way things are done is a just and centered one, but the momentum is not yet with you. You must bide your time. Be ready to seize the moment when it comes.

Change in the second line: Seize the day. Set things right.

Your time has come. Only delay and indecision can defeat you now. An opportunity to step into the moment presents itself. This revolution is like a merry-go-round that you yourself have set in motion. Now that it's up to speed, it is imperative that you step into the change and move with it. Allow it to carry you forward. The moment owns you; you must own it.

Change in the third line: A presumptive attack arouses a ghost lurking in the machinery. Wait. When the talk of revolution circulates again and again and yet again, then you can make your move.

Don't get ahead of yourself. There are powerful, unseen influences at work that have a vested interest in maintaining the status quo. If you want to change things, you will have to proceed slowly so as not to alert them to your intentions. When the momentum for change has gathered enough support that everyone — not just those in your own circle — are no longer whispering about it but clamoring for it, then you can act. If the matter is a private one, you need to nurture the support of your mind, your heart and your body. That is, you must be confident that your intellectual, emotional and physical energies are on board and up to the task.

Change in the fourth line: The spirit of the time is with you. No regrets. You have it in you to alter the course of your destiny.

Everything is in order. You have the endorsements you need at every level of being. What you do now changes everything.

Change in the fifth line: A person of integrity may undergo a public change of heart without humiliation or regret. Even before you roll the dice, you know the outcome.

The change indicated here is fundamental and inevitable. It can't be denied, disguised or hidden from view.

Change in the top line: With beautiful ferocity, the person of integrity changes body, mind and soul. The follower, meanwhile, gets a new tattoo.

There is a distinction to be made between changing the fundamental patterns of your life and changing your appearance to fit the prevailing mood. Revolution is not a fashion statement.

Superficial expressions of loyalty to a cause must sometimes be tolerated, but don't put your faith in branding that is only skin-deep. Symbols only carry power, they don't generate it.

50

The Sacred Pipe

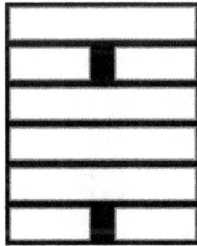

*"An elder once told me that tradition
only goes back one generation to the
person who taught you."*

*~ Keepers of the Sacred Tradition of
Pipemakers
(http://www.pipekeepers.org)*

Associated concepts, images and attributes: A sacred vessel, the
Holy Grail or communion cup, a cooking pot or cauldron, a
crucible or forge, a sacred meal or feast, personal or spiritual
transformation, a reorganization of the community or of the
individual at a higher level, self-actualization, gestation.

The Trigrams: Breath and Fire give rise to the image of a sacred pipe.

In Native American traditions, the bowl and stem of the sacred pipe, representing the female and the male, respectively, are carried separately, united only when the pipe is needed for a particular ceremony. Traditions and stories of the origin of the pipe vary from one people to another, but its purpose is always that of communion between the people, the earth, the sky and the four cardinal directions.

The sacred pipe carries implications for the individual in relation to the spiritual and social order. Tobacco and other herbs, barks and berries, as they are consumed in the bowl, give off aromatic smoke. Smoke is drawn into the mouth and puffed out again in each direction to signify the offerings of one who is to render service to humanity — whether to the family, the community or the world at large — and to acknowledge the divine mystery of the universe. In order to make such an offering, one must undergo a reorganization of the self and of one's priorities at the most fundamental levels of being, just as the female body makes adjustments to accommodate the needs of a growing fetus and the continuation of life. As a symbol of the sacred womb, the bowl suggests a place of spiritual gestation and transformation. The stem supports the bowl, and only when the two are ritually joined may the prayers of a sacred ceremony be uttered.

A time is indicated when individuality and selfish concerns give way to matters of greater importance in the form of service to one's community and in communion with divine mystery. This requires both clarity of mind with regard to one's purpose and a spirit of devotion penetrating enough to set aside any separatist agenda that might interfere with the provision of service to a cause that is deeper, higher and broader than the individual self.

Changing Lines

Change in the first line: The bowl is turned upside-down and the ashes knocked out so the pipe can be purified. Even a goddess menstruates.

While things might seem less than transformative at the moment, service is rendered nevertheless in ways that might appear rather ordinary. One maintains one's usefulness through regular practices of purification and cleanliness. Recognizing the sacred in the profane and the mundane is important to the preparation of the mind and necessary in order for the cycle of birth, death and rebirth to continue.

Change in the second line: There is tobacco in the bowl. No worries. The neighbor's envy cannot touch you.

When one undertakes to transform one's life, he or she often arouses resistance in the form of spite or jealousy in others. There is no need to be alarmed in such a situation, since no one can impede your progress. Regard it as a sign that the change in you is substantive and visible, and carry on.

Change in the third line: If the stem is broken, the ceremony cannot be performed. But rain falls, and remorse is spent. All goes well in the end.

There is substance and quality in what you are doing, but the means by which you might share it with others are ineffective. This is a sad state of affairs, and you may be inclined to grieve over it. If you can recognize and correct the problem, however, you can still be of service, and everyone will benefit.

Change in the fourth line: The pipe is not passed around the circle. Instead, the bowl is overturned, the fire goes out, and the pipe bearer is covered in ashes.

The basis for transformation is faulty when it manifests as either self-serving or careless. Instead of serving others, one spills the source of spiritual nourishment and validation by calling attention to oneself. This is wasteful, undignified and disrespectful to the community.

Change in the fifth line: A red clay pipe with a stem of carved cedar.

The cedar stem suggests that your gifts have found a means of expression that is as pleasing as the aromatic wood of the cedar. What you have to offer is accessible to others and can be shared in common. Hard work and continued effort will pay off.

Change in the top line: The sacred pipe is decorated with colored porcupine quills, gorgeously patterned, with a stem of carved ash.

You have something to offer that is not only useful but also precious and durable. Devote care to it for its own sake and also for the sake of its spiritual and symbolic value.

51

Quake

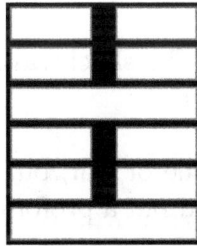

*The best place to be when the big one
hits is on the threshold, braced and
ready to move.*

Associated concepts, images and attributes: Trembling, shock,
reverberation, upheaval, earthquake, thunder, sudden and violent
movement, volatility, rapid pulse, adrenaline; invigorating,
arousing, fertilizing.

The Trigrams: Shock Repeated suggests an earthquake and its
repeated aftershocks.

Confronted by profoundly shocking or disturbing events, one is at
first unnerved. The physiological response to fear, however, is

identical to that of exhilaration; either state can be provoked by the same event. Two people in free-fall may feel the same bodily sensations, but one sees the racing pulse and involuntary shrieking as indicative of impending doom, while the other (the one with the parachute) is delighted to be having a peak experience. Interpretation is everything. Your situation is not defined by your visceral response to it; rather, you are free to define it on your own terms.

Maintain focus by maintaining composure. Do not be influenced by the panic of others. There are alternatives to the "fight or flight" response, but only a state of calm attentiveness allows one to recognize them and to capitalize on a situation that might send a less self-contained person fleeing in terror. The current upheaval is survivable. It changes everything, but you can ride it out.

Changing Lines

Change in the first line: The shockwave hits: quaking with fear, then shaking with laughter.

Your initial response is one of fear, but that will soon change to delight. This is not the end but a profound shift for the better. Go with it, let it change you!

Change in the second line: The quake hits and empties the bank vault. Everything is lost, but if you can climb to higher ground, your wealth will be restored to you.

Sudden and catastrophic events result in temporary loss. Do not try to rescue the situation; that would be like running into a building that is already crumbling. Instead, remove yourself to a place of calm and rest secure in the knowledge that, in time, you will realize how much you have gained in the process.

Change in the third line: Shaking and shaking. Wake up! It's time to get moving!

Something like this had to happen to jar you out of your indolence. Did you think you could sleep your life away? Get up and get on with your life! Use this startling new development to energize you. If you open your eyes, you'll see that it's not such a catastrophe.

Change in the fourth line: Shake yourself loose! Release yourself from the swamp!

You are bogged down in confusion, feeling stuck and overwhelmed. You need to shake things up if you want to get any traction. Surprise yourself. Do something out of character.

Change in the fifth line: Shock and aftershock. Reverberating ground makes it difficult to walk and exposes you to danger. Brace yourself in the middle of the doorway. You'll soon have plenty to keep you busy.

Things are coming at you from all sides, and the repeated upheaval threatens to throw you off balance. Remain poised and ready to move in either direction, forward or backward, depending on how it all shakes out, because when things slow down, you'll need to lend a hand to help pick up the pieces.

Change in the top line: The big one hits. Twisting and mangling. Wide-eyed terror everywhere. No chain-of-command; alliances and verbal agreements fall apart. If your neighbor has been hit, and not you, how is that your fault?

Widespread upheaval creates an atmosphere of utter panic. It is impossible, at such times, to orchestrate a response or to get people to co-operate, even for their own good. It might seem that you are only out to save your own skin, and in fact, that might be all you can do. Keep your wits about you, don't get caught up in the frenzy. Beware of people who let their fear get the better of them and of those who need to find someone else to blame for their misfortune.

52

Stillness

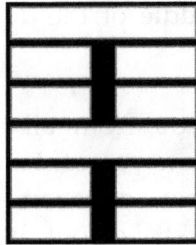

*It's hard to get through to a stone, and
just as difficult to put one over on a
mountain.*

Associated concepts, images and attributes: Stability, integrity,
self-assurance, stillness, tranquility, boundaries, immobility,
obstinacy.

The Trigrams: Mountain Repeated gives rise to ideas of serenity
and stillness, suggesting a state of sublime meditation.

Mountain ranges often represent natural boundaries between
nations, ecosystems and varieties of flora and fauna, climates and
weather patterns. The energy of stillness and self-containment
finds a convenient symbol in the immovability and tranquility of a

mountain. It is important, however, that we never mistake rigidity for self-reliance nor mere aloofness for an elevated state of mind.

The situation indicated here is one in which the need for activity has come to an end. This is a natural part of the cycle of life, the still point between inhalation and exhalation. It does not last forever — nothing does — but it carries with it a sense of timelessness and so it is not to be rushed. Resist the impulse to be *doing* and instead, content yourself with *being*. Collect yourself. Understand the natural limits of your own responsibility.

Changing Lines

Change in the first line: Keep your feet still. Hold your horses.

Resist acting impulsively just now. Do not take the step you are contemplating. Instead, pause long enough to allow the mind to grow quiet. Contemplating the situation from the vantage point of a relaxed detachment will free you from getting yourself needlessly entangled.

Change in the second line: Keep your calves still. There is no way to rescue a follower, though it breaks your heart.

The calves are the most well-developed muscles most people have, because they must always be on the move. Constantly chasing after an impossible ideal leads to bitter disappointment and dissatisfaction. If you recognize this in time, you can save yourself a great deal of trouble, but you can't save someone else who has fallen under the spell of a cultural dream. The pursuit of happiness can be a very sad game indeed, even for a spectator.

Change in the third line: Keeping the pelvis still causes the heart to smother.

Here stillness has turned into a form of asceticism or indolence that cuts you off from your true nature and threatens your emotional and physical health. The denial of basic human needs and desires ought not to be tolerated. Lighten up on yourself. Give yourself a little wriggle room.

Change in the fourth line: Keep the body still. The heart needs rest.

There is a difference between attempting to exert an artificial control over one's natural appetites and asserting mastery over obsessive or compulsive behavior. Here the heart is regulated and stabilized by the power of the mind. While this is not optimal, it is a step in the right direction and is entirely beneficial.

Change in the fifth line: Arresting the tongue. You have the right, and the insight, to remain silent.

Self-expression, too, has its natural limits. Words, because they are given so much power over the mental and social landscape, need to be moderated. When one is wholly aligned with one's purpose, then free speech will flow in a single direction and will not require inhibition. Until then, holding one's tongue is an option worth considering.

Change in the top line: A quiet heart is a generous heart.

When we understand the natural limits of need, responsibility and influence, it is possible at last to give without expectation of return or recognition. The heart that opens itself to love makes no distinction between giving and receiving. Abundance is abundance, whether it flows in or flows out.

53

The Suitor

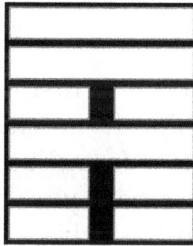

Action takes a longer path than words,
and kindness is slower to reveal itself
than wit or charm, but when strength
quietly and consistently practices the art
of gentleness, hearts migrate to one
another.

Associated concepts, images and attributes: Gentle persuasion, spiritual development, penetration, overcoming objections, courtship, engagement leading to marriage.

The Trigrams: Mountain and Wind represent the migration of geese over the mountains in spring, leading to warmer climates and mating grounds.

Gradual development relies on consistent, patient and persuasive effort in a single direction that neither pauses in its progress toward a goal nor skips any steps in the process. This means following form and convention, especially under conditions in which more abrupt or rash behaviors are likely to frighten, repel or confuse. The hexagram contains advice for one who courts a permanent connection or alliance based on mutual trust, affection and a commonality of interests. Gentleness and adaptability, honesty and honorable intentions are emphasized in the pursuit of an enduring commitment.

Changing Lines

Change in the first line: A young suitor steps onto the porch, flowers in hand. He must endure speculation and interrogation, but his intentions are faultless.

You are prepared to make the first move toward agreement, partnership or relationship. It is vital that you proceed in accordance with the expected formalities. A little charm will go a long way. You can expect to have your motives questioned in the beginning and to become the subject of gossip, but that is no reason to be deterred.

Change in the second line: Pairs of geese gather in the fields, eating and drinking at the shoreline.

The goose is a symbol of conjugal fidelity. Here, the vulnerabilities and insecurities of a new relationship or project have been overcome, and a lifelong bond has been established. Like geese flocking together in advance of the spring migration, you can enjoy a period of nourishing rest in the company of others, knowing that you will soon have more work to do and stiffer trials to face.

Change in the third line: Approaching the plateau, no turning back. The young and the weak are abandoned. The advantage lies in fighting off predators.

You are entering dangerous territory from which there will be no possibility of return. If you fail to heed the warning signs, you will be left high and dry. In the struggle for survival, you may feel abandoned or compelled to abandon something precious to you. Unless you can fight off attack after attack from those who would hijack them to their own ends, this spells a premature end to your plans.

Change in the fourth line: Rest and shelter are available at the sanctuary.

A sanctuary implies benevolent protection and influence. One's needs are provided for after a time of transition. There is no mistake in accepting such help, but the situation contains an implication of dangers yet to be faced. You have what you need for now, but your journey is not over.

Change in the fifth line: Gradually ascending to the sacred burial ground. The field lies fallow. Afterward, nothing can impede your development.

It is time to put the past respectfully to rest, allowing the unconscious processes to reintegrate that which appears to have been lost. The resulting period of infertility and apparent lack of creativity is essential to the progress of understanding and to the development of your ideas. You will not only get through this; in the end, you will come to honor and appreciate it as a time of restoration and rehabilitation that has led to greater achievement than might have been possible without such a period of mourning.

Change in the top line: The grey goose gradually disappears among the clouds. It drops a feather that might be worn in a sacred dance.

Gradual development leads us ultimately into the realm of the spirit. The transition is marked by the symbolic traces that one leaves behind. The work we do and the means by which we progress through the particular stages of life may serve as a guide to others who seek their own development. To continue in your own way is the best example you can offer to those who come after you.

54

The Auction Block

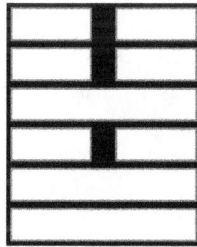

The slave keeps his head down and his heart steady. Chains restrict his limbs but not his mind or his spirit. Others decide his cost, but he alone determines his value.

Associated concepts, images and attributes: Duty without status, a lack of influence or power, circumstances beyond one's control.

The Trigrams: Metal and Movement suggest the image of a chain gang.

The situation indicated here is like that of a slave on the auction block, a prisoner in a chain gang, an enlisted soldier on a forced march or an employee without rank or seniority who is exposed to danger during a period of reorganization. In dealing with forces that lie beyond one's control, when there is little hope of escaping a situation unharmed, one is forced to submit to fate and allow oneself to be led. Since any attempt to manipulate events is doomed to failure, the course of action most likely to lead to success is simply to remain inwardly open and tractable, to lightly accept those duties that are required without putting oneself forward. Simply put, one is obliged to perform one's duties and to await the unfolding of a future in which an opportunity for greater power becomes available.

Changing Lines

Change in the first line: The universe is an equal opportunity employer. Handicapped, not disabled.

The fact that you have no position or power may seem like a serious handicap, but it does not restrict you from all possibility of advancement or accomplishment. The important thing is to perform those duties that are necessary and helpful, regardless of entitlement or the lack of it. By offering service of value to others you can bring true benefit to yourself as well.

Change in the second line: Shading the eyes, squinting in the sun. Keep a low profile.

Sometimes that which is glaringly obvious to everyone can blind us to important details that remain hidden or easily overlooked. It is especially important to one in an inferior role to maintain an independent perspective. Do not get caught up in the prevailing point of view. Keep to yourself and keep your own counsel.

Change in the third line: The mistress lets her hair grow out; the kept man grows a beard. Neither one can act like a spouse.

A situation that lacks public sanction is also lacking in the usual forms of power. Patience (like watching hair grow) and a certain self-abnegation are required. While a future settlement in one's favor may be implied, one may not presume upon it. Conditions at present remain tenuous. While no judgment is offered here, the inappropriateness of the situation must be taken into account.

Change in the fourth line: Letting the contract run out. Extending the deadline.

Forget about trying to bring things to a premature conclusion or settling for less than your true worth. Maintaining your independence, acting as a free agent for as long as necessary, will bring the recognition you deserve. Don't sell yourself short.

Change in the fifth line: The corner office goes to the junior partner. The senior, situated in the middle, has a view of the rising star.

The situation is full of promise in that it allows pride of place to go to one's subordinate while maintaining centrality for oneself. A choice is implied, since you have the power to demand certain privileges for yourself. But since real power has little to do with outward appearances, you may comfortably take a supporting role, promoting others who also have potential and are just coming into their own. "It is amazing what you can accomplish," said Harry Truman, "if you do not care who gets the credit."

Change in the top line: Raising an empty glass to make a toast. The cheeks are smiling, but not the eyes.

This is all form and no substance. Like the pleasantries of a subordinate who cannot speak freely, it means nothing and nothing meaningful will come of it.

55

The Zenith

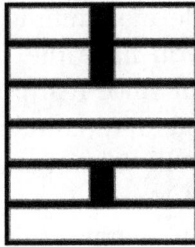

The sun doesn't need to know the time
of day, when to shine and when to quit.
The earth keeps track of the hours.

Associated concepts, images and attributes: The height of wealth and generosity. Plenty, copious growth, profusion, expansion, actualization, manifestation.

The Trigrams: Sun and Movement suggest midday and the approaching decline of afternoon. The movement may also indicate the passage of the moon in front of the sun, resulting in a solar eclipse.

The situation has reached its greatest expression, its maximum potential. Inevitably, this means that it will soon enter a period of decline. That is simply the way of things. The proper response, however, is to take joy in the moment and to share its blessing with commensurate generosity. Be like the midday sun. Radiate light and warmth. Take pleasure in your abundance and give abundantly to others. Express the fullness of your heart. Share knowledge, skill, wealth and joy.

Living in the moment is not the same as living for the moment. Nor is generosity to be confused with profligacy. The fully illumined mind is aware that good fortune does not last of its own accord. At the peak of good fortune, only an awareness of the cyclical nature of change will allow you to put your abundant resources to the best use.

Changing Lines

Change in the first line: Meeting a kindred spirit and staying for a week. A longer visit wears out your welcome.

You connect with something or someone—a meaningful task to which you are equal or a person of equal rank with whom you share a deep sense of recognition. In keeping with the time of abundance, you are encouraged to take full advantage of the opportunity while it lasts, but do not abuse it or allow it to become stifling or burdensome.

Change in the second line: The sun is eclipsed so that the Big Dipper is visible at noon. Doubts arise about how to proceed, but the omens are with you. Follow the shooting star.

Sometimes following your bliss means simultaneously facing your greatest fear. Just as you reach your maximum potential, so also your doubts abound, overshadowing your optimism and causing you to falter. Such darkness, however, allows you to see the monumental scale of things. Take the enormity of your fear as a sign of your imminent success. Allow it to guide you.

Change in the third line: The noonday sun is eclipsed so that even the individual stars of the Milky Way become visible. You've cut off your right hand, but it's not your fault.

In a time of abundance, a profusion of great and minor talents come to the fore, commanding attention. Inspiration can become overwhelming, enabling influences debilitating. You may not be able to accomplish much at the moment, but don't worry; the situation will evolve, and you will be able to assimilate the explosion of ideas and make use of them, all in good time.

Change in the fourth line: The noonday sun is eclipsed. The Big Dipper is visible. A clandestine meeting with a kindred spirit brings good news.

Doubts abound, but the situation is full of potential. You encounter something or someone with whom you share a deep connection and an instant sense of recognition. You can trust your instincts. Things that are hidden from the common view become readily apparent to you now.

Change in the fifth line: The sun's shafts break through. Brilliance and fame approach.

Like the re-emergence of the sun following an eclipse, this augers the visible return of one's inherent worth. The way forward is abundantly clear. Step into the light and share in a time of auspicious reward.

Change in the top line: Furnishing your own house, installing burglar alarms and motion detectors. No one shows up on your monitor.

A profound lack of trust will isolate you and turn a state of abundance into one of emotional poverty and paranoia. You have too much to offer to be acting this way. Jealously protecting what you have will leave you feeling robbed of so much more.

56

The Wanderer

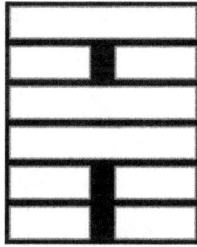

Unlike the fire in a hearth, a wildfire
consumes its fuel and moves on, or else
it dies.

Associated concepts, images and attributes: Wandering, travel, homelessness, lodging, sanctuary or temporary refuge, visiting away from home, a stranger in a strange land, expatriated, uprooted, a vagabond.

The Trigrams: Stone and Fire suggest a campsite or temporary shelter.

As members of a fundamentally social species, we long for inclusion. When we find ourselves outside our usual social frameworks, however, we are exposed to dangers that easily result from misunderstanding the mores of other groups.

Wandering, in this sense, may refer to a trip around the globe or around the corner. In fact, it is possible to venture beyond one's comfort zone these days with a laptop computer or a mobile phone.

The current situation is one in which one must negotiate difficult social terrain. In general, the advice is to remain tractable in behavior and attitude and attentive to social cues, to tread cautiously and to keep both the mind and the eyes wide open.

Social fitness means developing habits that promote mental flexibility. In a pluralistic society, cultural and moral rigidity makes us more than simply uncouth, it makes us vulnerable. When we cannot see around the corners of our own mental fortresses, we render our most cherished beliefs indefensible. In negotiating difficult or unfamiliar social terrain, strength resides in the recognition of ethical parity with others—even with one's enemies.

Changing Lines

Change in the first line: Nothing to live for. Nothing good will come my way.

Simply stated, what you are contemplating is a waste of your time and energy and it ends in self-defeat. Even if your ship rolls in, in your current frame of mind, you will simply watch it roll away again. You have more important things to do. Go tend to them.

Change in the second line: Coming to a campground with everything you need, you meet a young friend willing to help.

This is a good time to take a break. You have a proven record of self-reliance, but you don't always have to go it alone. It won't hurt to relax and enjoy the company of others. In fact, it will rejuvenate you.

Change in the third line: Burning your bed, setting fire to the inn. Who wants to travel with you now?

The violence of your passions threatens your own peace of mind. Worse than that, your disregard for the well-being of others constitutes a serious violation of their trust. Is it any wonder that you find yourself isolated? Keep going this way and you are likely to become a permanent outcast.

Change in the fourth line: A place to stay and money in the pocket. Still, the heart is restless.

You have acquired a certain level of comfort and responsibility, but it's not your place and it's not your responsibility. When you no longer follow your own path, dissatisfaction quickly sets in. There is more to life than this.

Change in the fifth line: The straight shooter takes down a pheasant with a single shot. Congratulations come with a pat on the back and the offer of a job.

Your aim is true, and your word is good. By proving yourself capable of handling a difficult situation with ease and efficiency, you earn both respect and greater responsibility.

Change in the top line: Setting fire to the attic and laughing about it. It seemed like a good idea at the time. What lessons can be learned from the ashes of a schoolhouse?

An intoxicating situation indeed; unfortunately, it has the power to trap you. There is nothing to be gained and everything to be lost. If you are looking for the end of the road, you've found a shortcut.

57

Digging

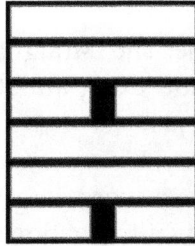

Proximity to sensitive information
determines whether an archaeologist
uses a backhoe, a shovel, a trowel, a
sifter or a brush to uncover the details of
the lives of others.

Associated concepts, images and attributes: Subtle penetration, permeation, infiltration, deliberation, percolation, absorption, capillary action, nourishment, grounding, gentleness, persistence.

The Trigrams: Penetration repeated gives rise to the idea of a shovel repeatedly, carefully and methodically penetrating the earth, suggesting an archeological dig.

The situation requires deliberative thought or mulling and the gradual accumulation of information and insight rather than a rush to judgment. Nothing sudden or forceful is likely to bring great benefit, neither a flash of revelation nor a leap of faith.

Subtle penetration to root causes and motivating factors, combined with compassion and a non-judgmental attitude will yield better, more accurate results.

Changing Lines

Change in the first line: Entrenchment. One step back, two steps forward. The resolute advance of a soldier is preferable.

Gentleness ought not to be confused with indecision. Success depends on mastering one's will and following through. It is possible to reverse a bad decision, but a failure to commit provides no results to evaluate. Course-correction is only possible after a course has been decided on. Take deliberate action.

Change in the second line: Digging under the bed. Using archeologists, physicians and metaphysicians of every stripe.

The situation is complicated by deceit and intrigue with its roots in the past. Unearth secrets, especially those of a sexual nature. Pay attention to your dreams, and make use of people whose skills include a variety of approaches to the problem, combining the insights of conventional as well as esoteric wisdom. People with insight into the deeper history of the situation provide invaluable assistance.

Change in the third line: Digging the same hole over and over again. It's exhausting.

Repeatedly pondering the same matter or asking the same question will not help you to delve any deeper into an issue, it only muddies the mind and inhibits your power. Similarly, seeking confirmation for a decision you have already made robs you of decisiveness and independence.

Change in the fourth line: Your worries are over. Three kinds of game are caught, and now you possess their attributes.

Catching game, in this context, suggests the careful study of a subject, its deep principles and sound practices. Three kinds of game mean that you have acquired the means by which to nourish yourself, to provide for others in the here and now, and to offer something of lasting practical and symbolic value to the world. You will not go wanting if you share generously with an eye to the welfare of future generations as well as your own.

Change in the fifth line: Wholly advantageous. Rain clouds disappear. A favorable wind for harvesting but not for planting. It blows for three days beforehand and three days after.

The situation clears up and drives away all doubt and worry. It's a good time to bring a project or plan to completion but not for starting something new. The three days beforehand suggest that you have ample time for finishing up; the three days after, that it is advisable to make a thorough assessment of the work once completed.

Change in the top line: Digging under the bed. Your diligence will cost you your shirt and your shovel.

This is not the time to delve into the past or to unearth anyone's deep, dark secrets—including your own. Even if you manage to dig something up, it will rob you of resources and dignity and impair your ability to discover more vital information later on.

58

Joy

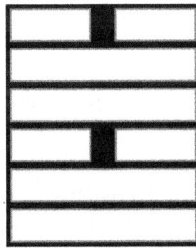

*My weapon is hammered joy, my shield
the naked truth. Even fear enlightens
me.*

Associated concepts, images and attributes: Delight, exuberance, pleasure, cheer, openness, expressiveness, humor, laughter, talking and smiling, communication, exchange of information or goods, business, the marketplace.

The Trigrams: Laughter Repeated suggests the infectious laughter of children and a deep and abiding sense of joy in life.

We are reminded that the way to participate fully in life is by giving and receiving joy with both hands wide open. This is possible regardless of one's circumstances, but only to the extent that we recognize the true basis of joy, that it resides not in the mindless pursuit of pleasure but in acting in accordance with the laws of nature that give rise to it.

As an expression of pure delight, laughter is infectious and beneficial. So much so that it has been used as an instrument of healing. It is also a weapon that can be used to great effect for the purpose of self-defense, for displaying the weaknesses of an argument or belief and for the deflation of the ego—especially one's own.

Changing Lines

Change in the first line: An open face. Spontaneous laughter.

The connection is genuine and trustworthy. You may express yourself fully without worry or doubt. Don't hold back.

Change in the second line: Laughing together dispels illusions and allows the truth to emerge.

When a relationship is based fundamentally in the joy of mutual association, doubts about one another's motives simply vanish. You have made a contact that will open your mind and your heart like a revolving door, allowing pleasure to come and go perpetually, without fear or reservation.

Change in the third line: Employing laughter as an import/export business. Gag gifts and pratfalls.

Idle pleasures that come from without amuse us, but often without providing any lasting or nourishing effect. When a connection is lacking in sincerity, it provides no net gain in energy and in fact may lead to a leakage of joy. Laughter at the expense of others expresses no joy in life; rather it exposes one's fear of it.

Change in the fourth line: Weighing the pros and cons. Tip the balance in favor of harmony and you will increase your joy.

You are treating the situation as a business deal in which everyone is looking out solely for his or her own interests, so no one comes out ahead. It is up to you to change the dynamic. Stop trying to win and negotiate instead for mutual benefit and agreement. Don't just sweeten the deal; make it nourishing. This will increase your own satisfaction.

Change in the fifth line: There may be honor among thieves, but you will still be robbed of joy.

You feel a certain connectedness to a disturbing and detrimental element. If you honor it, you will end up dishonored and distrusted, because you must compromise a more fundamental and universal set of values in order to fit in. The resulting tension is a constant drain on your well-being, your effectiveness, and your happiness. Making the right choice is crucial.

Change in the top line: The lady or the tiger?[1] You open the door to a permanent influence—whether to seduction or addiction isn't clear yet.

Love is a risky business. You are flirting with something that will stake a claim and make demands. Keep your eyes and your mind open. This could represent a lasting source of joy and pleasure; it might just as easily skin you alive. You can turn away from it and accept the fact that you will never know, or you can open the door and find out.

---

[1] In the much anthologized short-story "The Lady or the Tiger" by Frank R. Stockton, a king, upon discovering that his daughter has received the attentions of a suitor unworthy of her station, forces the young man in question to appear in the arena, or gladiator ring, where he must choose between two doors. Behind one door waits a beautiful woman to wed him; behind the other, a ferocious tiger to eat him. The young man, either foolishly or wisely, looks to the princess for help. The princess, knowing which is which, obligingly indicates one of the two doors. The story ends with the young man's fate undecided.

59

Dissolving

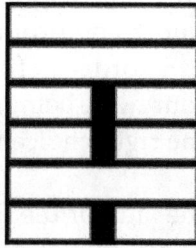

*When lion weather roars retreat and
northerly retracts the claw of winter, the
lambs come out to play again.*

Associated concepts, images and attributes: Dispersing solids; removing obstacles; dissolving differences, resistance or interference; dispelling illusions and misunderstandings; eliminating rigidity; scattering; disintegrating; undermining.

The Trigrams: Ice and Wind suggest the image of a spring thaw, when the steady influence of a warm breeze breaks up the ice that has blocked the normal flow of a river for an extended period of time.

When we meet with resistance due to misunderstanding, distrust, or mental and emotional rigidity, forcefulness is often counter-productive. A steady and consistent warmth is required in order to break up an underlying fear or doubt. Answer objections patiently; dissolve misunderstanding with honest and gentle explanation.

Often, the most stubborn obstacles a person faces are those that have accumulated unawares within one's own heart and mind. Beliefs and attitudes that have built up over a lifetime cannot be removed in a day. Compassion begins with the self, the ego. Only by understanding the true nature of our own fears can we eliminate the need for their protection. Just as in dealing with the misunderstandings of others, patience and genuine warmth directed inward is more effective than a harsh and demanding attitude.

Changing Lines

Change in the first line: Horse sense to the rescue. A fortunate intervention.

The horse is a symbol of strength and speed combined with gentleness. Here at the outset, before misunderstandings have a chance to harden into opposition and entrenchment, a certain strength of mind is useful in setting things straight. Because the situation isn't complicated, it can be resolved simply and quickly.

Change in the second line: The ice cracks like thunder. Run like the wind. Find solid ground.

During a time of dissolution, temporary alliances that have formed for mutual protection against a common threat begin to fall apart. It is vital that you move quickly at the first sign of discord to find the support of a community of interests based on more fundamental principles.

Change in the third line: When the ice thaws, the flow is re-established.

Here, the disintegration of the ego is indicated. When you identify with the flow of energy in relationship rather than with your own side or part in it—with the work to be done rather than the credit to be taken and the profit or power to be gained from it—then you are able to move effectively and to accomplish something worthwhile.

Change in the fourth line: Dissolving the school on the steps of the library. You don't have to go into hiding, but you need a place to think.

You have an opportunity to develop a greater understanding of yourself, of humanity and of the world than is afforded by a particular dogma or creed. This means separating yourself from your former associates, not because you are ashamed, but because you need a certain distance from them in order to think for yourself. This is not a mistake. What might once have seemed like heresy will bring you greater clarity and more resilient convictions.

Change in the fifth line: Breaking out in a sweat. Raise your voice and dissolve the deadlock.

This is like a fever breaking. Something has gone seriously wrong, but if you can bring the situation to a head, it will readily dissolve. You may have to make a lot of noise in order to call attention to the problem, but so be it. It can no longer be ignored.

Change in the top line: Dissolving bad blood. If you go into exile you can emerge again without shame.

It is up to you to remove the cause of conflict, even if it means removing yourself. There is no mistake in doing this, since it spells the end of a cycle of negativity and allows you to make a fresh start elsewhere. Sometimes, the easiest way to change your environment is to find a more suitable one.

60

Articulation

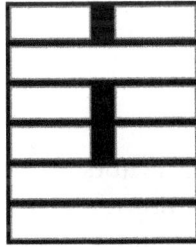

*Beavers create ecosystems by the
articulation of streams to make ponds to
accommodate their lodges; by the
manipulation of tiny streams of air to
produce speech, humans articulate ideas
and have transformed an entire planet.*

Associated concepts, images and attributes: Making distinctions, breaking down or separating into units or parts, connecting joints, clear and concise expression of thoughts, categories, units of time, divisions, chapters, nodes, cells or pods, laws, regulations, limits, boundaries, confinement.

The Trigrams: Lake and Water give rise to the image of a body of water contained by the natural features of a landscape or by the introduction of a dam.

Coherent thought and communication require a certain level of organization or separation into discreet elements of time and space as well as into categories. While such divisions might seem arbitrary and counter to the idea of experience as a continuous flow, they are necessary in order to facilitate survival.

You are asked, in the present circumstance, to pay particular attention to the organization of people, places, items and events and to regulate behavior. Articulate your thoughts, acquire precision without abandoning fluidity, develop mastery of yourself and your environment without resorting to tyranny.

Changing Lines

Change in the first line: Confining yourself to your own quarters is not a mistake.

Bide your time. External factors are so convoluted that they prevent any effective solution or meaningful involvement. Stay out of it by keeping to yourself.

Change in the second line: Confining yourself to your own house and yard is unfortunate. You risk losing a significant opportunity.

Once the impediments to action have been removed, don't wait for opportunity to come knocking. Go out and greet it. Your time is now, but if you let it slip by, it will belong to someone else.

Change in the third line: A lack of discipline means no lack of tears.

If you want to be effective, you must set yourself in order. If you don't, you will regret it.

Change in the fourth line: Appreciating one's limits means that steady development is possible.

A profound sense of realism allows for contentment regardless of one's circumstances. Contrary to conventional thinking, which would have one straining against all obstacles, the ability to acknowledge and indeed enjoy one's true abilities means that one can make the best possible use of them. Contentment, in this sense, is the key to a productive life.

Change in the fifth line: Refreshingly articulate. Continue, esteemed colleague.

You express your wishes and intentions eloquently, allowing others to grasp your ideas immediately. This leads not only to greater understanding but to greater respect and consideration.

Change in the top line: Bitter discipline plants the seeds of disappointment.

Imposing harsh limitations leads to resentment, resistance and revolt. This applies to unnatural restrictions placed on the behavior of others as well as to extreme forms of self-denial.

61

Integrity

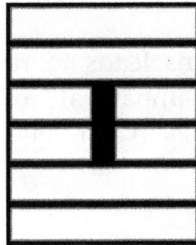

*When we speak and act in accordance
with our original nature, which is at
once both innocent and wise, nothing
that we say or do can be held against us.
We stand grounded in the fundamental
joy of knowing who we are.*

Associated concepts, images and attributes: Spiritual grounding, centering, intuitive knowledge, self-assurance, moral compass, fulcrum, balance, stability, accord between one's inner and outer lives, self-actualization.

The Trigrams: Lake and Wood suggest a secluded environment, deep waters self-contained and undisturbed by the prevailing winds.

The concept of personal integrity means more than, but not less than, keeping faith with one's word. We generally hear it applied in the backward and inside-out sense of sticking by what has been said, of keeping promises. While this is an important subsection of the social contract, it is far more important to abide by the agreements one makes with oneself, to follow one's inner compulsion toward full self-expression, so that the words that issue from our mouths and the actions performed by our hands find resonance in our personal truths.

Changing Lines

Change in the first line: Diligent preparation leads to a good outcome. If you grasp the matter firmly, you may disregard the opinions of others.

Two things are important here: that you consult with yourself and yourself alone on the matter at hand and that you bring it into harmony with your central purpose. When you grasp it as an integrated expression of who you are, what others think, do or say about it will be of no particular concern to you.

Change in the second line: Like one crane calling out from the shade to another. My cup is overflowing, come share it with me!

The profound recognition of one kindred spirit by another occurs spontaneously as a heartfelt call and response. Give voice to your feeling, and those who share it will be attracted to you. You won't have to seek them out; they will answer of their own accord.

Change in the third line: You've met your match on a roller coaster ride. Maybe you raise your hands in the air; maybe you hang on tight. Maybe you laugh, maybe you scream.

The "match" indicated here is your equal, your mate, but it also suggests an opponent. You engage in a contest that goes back and forth with no promise of decisive victory or defeat. Your struggle is like a difficult marriage—on again, off again, with more than its share of highs and lows. When things go your way, you celebrate; when they turn against you, you mourn. No judgment or advice is offered here, because the question of winning or losing is irrelevant. The struggle maintains the relationship and vice versa. To quit the one is to quit the other.

Change in the fourth line: Under a waxing gibbous moon, the team horse runs away. There is no one to blame.

Although the situation is not yet fully illuminated, there is enough light by which to negotiate a path. The breakdown of a partnership is suggested, but no fault is attached to the one who acts independently to break ties with the other, nor to the one who is left behind. Each will be able to find a way to move on alone.

Change in the fifth line: This is acting with integrity. It allows you to operate as if under contract with the divine.

Standing firmly on your own ground, you have found a way to connect deeply with the spirit of the time. Act with the courage of your convictions. You render true service to the world.

Change in the top line: The cock crows to high heaven. Words die on the wind.

A rooster makes a lot of noise, but its wings are clipped. When there is no real connection between intention and ability or between words and deeds, one loses the trust of others and, ultimately, faith in oneself.

62

Flying Low

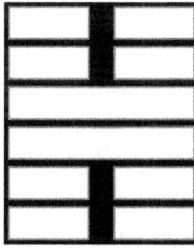

The need to grandstand is incompatible with a life on the run.

Associated concepts, images and attributes: Extreme caution, attention to detail, smallness, ineffectuality; fleeting, fugitive.

The Trigrams: Stillness and Motion, by the arrangement of weak and strong lines, suggest the image of a small, low-flying bird beating its wings furiously while keeping its body still.

During a time of transition or flight from captivity or danger, when things are up in the air, so to speak, it is generally unwise to expose oneself to view. Since a multitude of details must be dealt with fastidiously, little time or attention is left for big ideas or projects. This is as it should be. Stay under the radar for now. Life may seem a bit drab, even melancholy, at the moment, but that, too, is to be expected. The way to get through the ordeal is to devote yourself to small, ordinary tasks as they crop up, without becoming discouraged. Even if you had it in you to put up a herculean struggle, you would not succeed. It is better for now to keep your head down.

Changing Lines

Change in the first line: The bird on the wing takes the buckshot.

Stay put, stay low, keep your feet on the ground and your head on your shoulders. Any abrupt attempt to escape the situation will bring disaster.

Change in the second line: Don't knock on the president's door; instead, go to the secretary's desk. The little people are of more help to you than the big kahuna.

Staying low means regarding nothing and no one as beneath you. Show respect for the gatekeepers and others who occupy positions of secondary importance. Be willing to accept a supporting role yourself. Now is not the time to seek the limelight, but that does not mean that you can't make real progress toward your objectives. In fact, by forging connections at the level where the machinery gets oiled and the grunt work gets done, you will accomplish a great deal that otherwise might get overlooked.

Change in the third line: You stretch out your neck and wonder why the axe is falling.

You have exposed yourself to real danger. It is too late to pull back, and there is no way to go forward. The best you can hope for is to fend off the attack when it comes.

Change in the fourth line: While in flight, push on only as far as you must. The bloodhounds will pass you by. If you try to finish the journey, they will finish you.

The crisis is over, at least temporarily. You meet an unexpected opportunity to escape from danger but only if, when you reach a stopping point, you stop. That which has been dogging you will lose interest in you if you let it. If you ignore this warning and try to press on or bring things to a conclusion, you will only put yourself in greater danger.

Change in the fifth line: A shroud of fog blows in from the west, but no rain falls. A grappling hook catches the caveman.

A pervasive lack of clarity offers concealment but no opportunity to distill the facts of the situation or to provide satisfaction or release from tension like that brought about by a cleansing downpour. Nevertheless, by grappling with ancient or ancestral traditions, or by seeking out one who has retreated from the world at large, you gain access to wisdom that would otherwise remain hidden from you.

Change in the top line: The high-flying bird makes a brilliant target. Bagged and tagged.

Given the need for extraordinary caution, you overestimate your ability to bring the transition to a successful conclusion. Through arrogance and a need to call attention to yourself, you overshoot your mark. Only the attempt is grand; the end result is small and mean, of importance only to the statistician.

63

Momentum

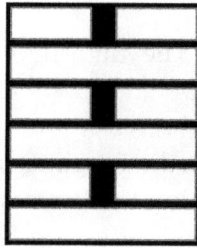

When you throw your heart at a goal,
your head and your hands will follow.

Associated concepts, images and attributes: In motion, a work in progress, under way, continual effort, consistent achievement, full steam ahead, forward progress.

The Trigrams: Fire and Water show each of the strong, or odd-numbered, lines and each of the weak, or even-numbered, lines in a corresponding position in the hexagram, giving rise to the idea that everything has found its place and is in working order.

Since everything is properly set up and the matter under consideration has already been set in motion, success now depends on forging ahead. Arbitrarily shifting weight or changing direction in mid-stride will cause you to stumble; yet it is vital, in a fluid situation, that you remain adaptable to emerging crises and deal with them effectively. Stay with the process and keep moving forward. Keep your long-term goals in mind, but do not try to accomplish everything at once or to reach a conclusion or culmination prematurely. The constant challenges, shifting currents and uncertain footing all serve to keep you on your toes. By responding in the moment, you remain at the height of your creative powers and in the state of flow.

Changing Lines

Change in the first line: Horns blare from behind, but the light hasn't changed yet. If your foot is on the brake and you get rear-ended, you are not at fault.

At the beginning of an enterprise, do not allow the anxieties of others to propel you into action prematurely. The time to begin will announce itself. You may suffer criticism, back-biting and even minor damages as a result of a general atmosphere of impatience, but you will not err in sticking to your guns. Recognize patience as your virtue.

Change in the second line: The ball is low and outside. Don't chase it. The one on the mound will have to pitch to you eventually.

Remaining adaptable in a fluid situation doesn't mean reaching after every so-called opportunity that's pitched to you. When the right thing comes your way, it will be within your reach, and you will connect with it. Wait for it. Let it come to you.

Change in the third line: Expansion means competition on all sides. In due time, you will prevail. Employ no one who is incapable of sharing your vision.

You have undertaken something that of necessity requires the time and energy of others to accomplish. In spite of outside interference and competition for resources, the likelihood of your long-term success is strong. However, if you rely on people who are primarily self-interested, you will be hindered at every turn, and your efforts undermined.

Change in the fourth line: A riches-to-rags story, unfortunately. Still, old clothes are good for plugging leaks and wiping up spills. Be careful from sunup to sundown.

Forward progress has stalled out. A set of once great and innovative ideas has become old hat, but even so, they are not entirely useless. Find ways to reuse, repurpose or recycle them. You can bring a project to completion even if it lacks its former allure. But in working with dilapidated ideas, equipment or other resources, a greater than usual sense of precaution and alertness is necessary. The situation is fraught with problems and potential for sapping you of energy and enthusiasm, but it is not yet a lost cause.

Change in the fifth line: The poor widow's two cents are worth more than the endowment of a wealthy contributor.[2]

Simply put, sincerity and conviction more than make up for a lack of resources. A big investment for the purpose of making an impression or convincing yourself or others that you care does little to fill the need. You are asked to give your all, not merely what you think you can afford or what is expected. This is not a time for calculating the return on your investment.

Change in the top line: In too deep. Over your head.

Having pushed on too far and too fast, with too little forethought or awareness of danger, you risk losing everything. You do not have the means to prevail in this situation. If you do not turn back now, you will fail utterly.

---

[2] Mark 12:41-44, Luke 21:1-4. In a lesson to his disciples, Jesus points out the value of a small sacrifice on the part of a poor but sincere widow compared to that of a wealthy donor's ostentatious contribution.

64

Incubation

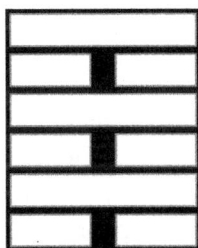

In the early stages of creation, nothing is
certain; everything is fluid and chaotic.
Then suddenly, with the rapid
expansion of a strong central idea, order
comes into being, the first elements
coalesce, and a new universe is born.

Associated concepts, images and attributes: Confusion, chaos, disorganization, the primordial soup, preconscious processing, dreaminess, creative reverie or brooding, anticipation.

The Trigrams: Water and Fire suggest the sudden appearance of light out of darkness, order out of chaos, the cosmos out of the singularity of no-space and no-time. In this arrangement, the alternating weak and strong lines occupy opposing positions in the hexagram (even-numbered lines in odd-numbered positions and vice versa), giving rise to the idea that nothing has found its appropriate place. The key concept, however, is that of *not-yetness*, of gearing up and getting organized for something momentous. It is with this sense of expectancy that the cycle of hexagrams comes to a close and prepares to begin again.

A state of apparent inactivity often precedes a burst of creativity. Outwardly, this may seem like laziness, dreaminess, or inertia; but inwardly, one has at least a vague sense that something new is brewing. It is important not to rush this inner work, nor is it wise to move directly into production mode without laying the groundwork for it. First, the conscious mind needs to be clued in, goals formulated and resources gathered. Levels and degrees of pre-planning vary greatly from individual to individual and from project to project. Micro-management might hamstring one undertaking, while a lack of organization allows the energy for another to dissipate.

The changing lines take their imagery from the idea of a creative journey, road trip or race. In general, the early indication is that you are not yet ready to make a move. Particularly in the lower lines of change, which represent danger, restraint combined with a continued mulling of a central idea or problem is advised. More needs to be done in the way of preparation before you can set out effectively. The upper lines represent a greater clarity of purpose and therefore indicate success.

Changing Lines

Change in the first line: Tires spinning in the mud, fishtailing, the tail lights end up in the ditch.

Impetuousness will spell the end of your plans. Your eagerness to be underway, combined with a lack of insight regarding the conditions you will meet once you begin, cause you to lose control and promptly remove you from the course of action you intend to pursue.

Change in the second line: There's gas in the tank, but the light hasn't changed. Keep your foot on the brake.

You are prepared, and you have sufficient energy for the undertaking, but external conditions are not yet right. Bide your time. Everything looks promising. By mastering your own impulsive drives in the beginning, you gain mastery of the situation for the long haul.

Change in the third line: Before setting out, micro-management cripples. Test the waters, collect the evidence.

You want to make sure that everything is perfect before you begin, but that is, by definition, impossible. Make a move. Test your ideas in the rough and tumble world outside your own head, outside the laboratory or boardroom, and pay attention to the initial results. Let real-world tests provide the feedback you need. Then you will know how to continue.

Change in the fourth line. A trial run shows great promise. No worries. A surprise attack leaves them staring after you. A long string of successes lies ahead.

The early signs are favorable. The time for hesitation is past. Move quickly and you are assured of a stunning victory. This is a transformative development with lasting repercussions.

Change in the fifth line: A trial run is successful. No worries. Brilliance lights the way forward.

All signs are go. The road ahead is wide open and well-lit. Your success is a reflection of your inner worth and sincerity. Give to the future with both hands.

Change in the top line: Trophy in hand, drinking champagne. When they tip the cooler over your head, you can forget all about it.

When the moment of celebration comes at long last, then and only then can you relax and forget about the difficulties of the past. It is important to mark your successes well; it is more important to leave them behind you. Here at the end of the entire cycle of changes represented by the sixty-four hexagrams of the Book of Changes, the time comes around to start again. Congratulations! Your trials are over! Celebrate and move on. The trial is soon to begin.

HEXAGRAM LOCATOR

UPPER TRIGRAM →

LOWER TRIGRAM ↓

2	23	8	20	16	35	45	12
15	52	39	53	62	56	31	33
7	4	29	59	40	64	47	6
46	18	48	57	32	50	28	44
24	27	3	42	51	21	17	25
36	22	63	37	55	30	49	13
19	41	60	61	54	38	58	10
11	26	5	9	34	14	43	1

A hexagram is built from the bottom up. The first three lines form the lower trigram, which you will find in the vertical column to the left of the grid. Lines four through six determine the upper trigram, which you will find in the horizontal row at the top of the grid. Follow the row of the lower trigram until it intersects with the column of the upper trigram, and you have your hexagram.

ABOUT THE AUTHOR

Ien Nivens is an artist and an educator by training and a seeker by inclination. He grew up in Oklahoma and moved to New England in 1980. He lives in the Berkshire Mountains of Western Massachusetts with his wife Michelle and a cat named Barnaby. He works as a web and graphic design consultant for artists and musicians at Socialcopter. His book reviews and reviews of art, music and performance appear online at http://artslashlife.com and http://www.berkshirefinearts.com.

Mr. Nivens is currently writing a fantasy novel called *The Likener* and an American gothic novel called *Earthworm Soup*.

For more information about divination using *The American Book of Changes* and for instructions in making a set of custom dice for throwing hexagrams or to order a set made just for you, please visit http://theamericanbookofchanges.com

www.ingramcontent.com/pod-product-compliance
Lightning Source LLC
Chambersburg PA
CBHW071335090426
42738CB00012B/2908